## Other Works by This Author

*The 4 Secrets of the Universe*

*The Book of Manifesting*

*Mysteries, Prophecies, and the Hollow Earth*

*Poems of Life, Love,
and the Meaning of Meaning*

*Poet Gone Wild*

*Sojourn*

*The Lightness of Being*

### *Infinite Healing Trilogy*

*Poems and Messages for the
Loss of a Loved One*

*Poems and Messages for the
Loss of Your Animal Companion*

*Healed in Timelessness*

# All About

*the*

# Soul's Journey

*Understanding Death*

PAUL GORMAN

Copyright © 2024 Paul J. Gorman
All Rights Reserved

 Year of the Book
135 Glen Avenue
Glen Rock, PA 17327

ISBN 13: 978-1-64649-467-5 (print)
ISBN 13: 978-1-64649-468-2-8 (ebook)

Cover photo by author, Western Maryland
Interior images licensed by iStockphoto.com unless otherwise noted.

No part of this publication may be reproduced, distributed, or transmitted in any form or by any means, including photocopying, recording, or other electronic or mechanical methods, without the prior written permission of the author, except in the case of brief quotations embodied in critical reviews and certain other noncommercial uses permitted by copyright law.

Library of Congress Control Number: 2024924087

Some names have been altered to retain privacy.

Note to reader: This book contains channeled information from people I knew that have died. It is presented here in the order it was received, with no content omissions.

## Contents

Foreword .................................................................. 1
Introduction ............................................................. 2
Hillen ....................................................................... 4
Ray ........................................................................ 11
Pete ....................................................................... 13
Hillen Again ......................................................... 18
Jackie ................................................................... 22
Dave & Russell .................................................... 30
Hillo ...................................................................... 35
Wayne .................................................................. 39
Buck ..................................................................... 45
Holly ..................................................................... 51
Marty .................................................................... 55
Lynda ................................................................... 60
Dad ....................................................................... 63
Rich ...................................................................... 67
Loriann ................................................................. 73
Billy & John ......................................................... 83
Peter Giampietro & Mr. Coe ................................ 87
Loriann Again ...................................................... 91
Eric ....................................................................... 96
Lulo .................................................................... 100
Loriann, Billy & John ........................................ 102
   *Dorothy Gale* ................................................ 106
   *It Depends What You See* ........................... 114
Afterword ........................................................... 118
   *God's Only Plan* ........................................... 120
About the Author ............................................... 122

"But it wasn't a dream—it was a place!—and you, and you, and you—and you were there!

But you couldn't have been, could you?... This was a real, truly live place, and I remember that some of it wasn't very nice-—but most of it was beautiful!

But just the same, all I kept saying to everyone is 'I want to go home', and they sent me home!"

—Dorothy in *The Wizard of Oz* closing scene

## Foreword

Spirits of deceased people can provide us with a wealth of information about the spirit world, and about our continued journeys after our lifetimes on Earth. This book has detailed accounts of lifetime ending events from people who have died—and more importantly, what happened to them next after death.

My previous books are conversations with God, and also with different advanced beings about the nature of reality.

Until now, I was never interested in connecting with spirits of deceased people, thinking that they would be about as reliable as living people. Now I know that is incorrect.

They are healed minds, having left their bodies and egos behind. Their spirits are aware in their energy bodies.

The channeled information in this book gives us their spirits' perspectives of life, and of death—helping us to understand it.

## Introduction

What is it like to die? I'd like to know, but I don't want to find out.

This book explores death in conversations with those who have passed away. They have related to me what dying was like for them—and then what happened after that.

I recommend reading this book only after you have allowed sufficient time to heal from a recent loss—maybe even a few years.

My book, *Infinite Healing: Poems and Messages for the Loss of a Loved One,* is more intended for healing a recent loss. It can be helpful for processing the shock, grief, sadness and anger as you heal in time, and allow more of the happy memories into your thoughts.

Death is the one thing that all of life has in common. Our instincts for self-preservation are always on alert to avoid it. The finality of death is in the back of our minds as the worst thing that could happen.

Our fear from not knowing "when, how, why, and then what?" make it even more frightening. It is often considered a tragedy, sometimes natural, but only rarely as our own healing decision.

That would certainly give new meaning to the term "free will."

The more years we do live, the more times death hits close to home—until eventually it does hit home.

What if it is a beautiful experience—to finally be free of limitations, pain, and suffering—both physical and mental?

Our lifetimes are for healing. We each have a purpose and healing objectives. My messages say that we heal in life, or in the moment our lives end—but either way, we will heal. The mind and spirit do not die. Only the temporary body dies.

See what others who have passed away say in the chapters ahead. They are all people I knew, and I appreciate that they have shared their experiences here. Their reports and insights from the spirit world are fascinating, giving us valuable information about life's biggest mystery. Here are their perspectives from the other side.

Are we in a dream while our spirits are in reality? Are our lives, families, challenges, and lifetime endings chosen by us for a purpose—and agreed upon by all involved?

Let's talk all about the soul's journey—understanding death.

## Hillen

**Can I speak with my friend Hillen who passed away 1 year ago?**
*Yes, allow him to hear your mind speaking to him.*

**Hello Hillen.**
*Happy to hear from you again Paul!*

**I am sad that you had passed away—you were totally fit and not very old.**
*A lifetime ending can be any moment you choose for it to be, and however you can find an ending to it.*

**Spirits of people often prompt me that they had died. Did you prompt me with the news?**
*Yes, I did, meaning I heard you asking about me.*

**Can I ask you why you chose to leave the planet?**
*All of my lifetime goals had been achieved, making it an easier decision for me.*

**By our measures, you had it all—looks, personality, prosperity, family, health, etc.**
*All except healing my homesickness for all in my spiritual home.*

**So, you chose cancer to bring your life to a close?**
*I chose cancer because it forced my family to hear me, all together as a family.*

**Did you want them to know that you love them?**
*They already know that I love them. I wanted all of them to hear me tell them things from my heart, for them to hear only.*

**I am sorry that you are gone. The world was a better place with you in it.**
*Ha! I am laughing.*

**My favorite thing about our long-distance commuting was the time we spent together.**
*A commute that I enjoyed also, meaning in your company.*

**I am still a fortune-teller as you called me, but more into writing books about the nature of reality.**
**Can you tell me about your journey out of this life?**
*A lifetime ending can be however it is most advantageous for each person, such as me having family with me.*

*Altering health meant not allowing my body to assimilate nutrients, and to allow a medical intervention to kill me.*

**Would it be considered not loving yourself to allow your body to get sick and die?**
*A healthy body means having a healthy mind, or one that is not homesick. A homesick mind has a sick body that will be going home.*

**You said you had "homesickness for all in my spiritual home." Did you return to your soul group?**
*All are here in my groups, and I am happy here.*

**We'll talk about that, but I'd like to start at the beginning—or what we consider the ending. What did you experience before you passed away?**
*I accepted ending life as I knew it, and angels came all around me in the hospital bed. I acknowledged a guardian angel that had always been near me in my life. All healed in my mind as we discussed the life I had chosen to learn from.*

*We had a long discussion in terms of finding healing in all of my thoughts in love, and in peace.*

*All of a sudden, I had a flash of light in my mind that could not be brighter, making all of my lifetime concerns evaporate in it.*

*Acclimating to that brightness, I was then heading into it myself—meaning I must have died at that point.*

*A long, illuminated hollow tube opened up in the top of my head, and I was pulled into it. After I entered it, half of my body was not going to be with me any longer, meaning my physical body. My light body had become my healed body.*

*As I left the Earth, I could see I was getting farther away from it as I headed into the Earth light ring of all consciousness.[1]*

*In the Earth ring of consciousness, I could be all that God promised me at my inception—all lovingness, gentleness, and peacefulness.*

**Were you greeted by other beings or predeceased relatives after you died?**
*A lot of people I knew helped me to acclimate after I arrived in the Earth ring of consciousness.*

**How many people?**
*About 8 or 9 people I knew in my lifetime.*

**Were some family members?**
*All had been family except one friend from high school, and he acclimated me the most, being here the longest.*

**Is there a sense of time duration there?**
*Allowing a time sequence heals in the mind only- not in the Mind of God, encompassing all in an instant.*

**What did you have to acclimate to?**
*A thought manifests instantly, so keep them only on healing.*

**Does the spirit need to continue healing after a life?**

---

[1] Discussed in my book, *Sojourn*.

*A spirit has healing homework to do—as a lifetime heals, a spirit life also heals. A spirit heals itself in its home in all consciousness.*

*Healed in eternity is the home of the spirit.*

**Are spirits healing or healed?**
*All are healing in their minds, and healed in the Mind of God, so they are both—at the same healing and healed point in the Mind of God.*

**Did you have an initial period of introspection when entering the spirit world?**
*Acclimating had an initial period of introspection which heals the most after completing a lifetime. There is guidance there to help you assimilate the lessons.*

**Then did you join your group?**
*I joined my groups in the first few minutes after leaving the Earth. All of them had a homecoming for me, making all of my homesickness heal and go away.*

**I am sure you enjoyed it.**
*Actually, I enjoyed it more than I loved my lifetime enjoyments, like when we had drinks in the club at The Breakers.*

**I have a fond memory of that.**
*All fond memories are nothing like the atmosphere here. It is like a long and enjoyable hot bath in love and peacefulness.*

**What do you intend to do next—rejoin your groups?**

*I am always heading from one group to another, making all of my activities about healing.*

**Can you please tell me about the nature of your soul groups?**
*All of my groups allow me to heal all that I can think of—meaning all of the Earth life feelings of insecurity and lack of trust in God, and myself as God's mindful son losing his mind, basically.*

**I hear ya.**
*Hearing in the mind is your great skill.*

**You confirmed my belief that the best people leave first, giving the rest of us plenty of time!**
*Ha! I am laughing, Gorman!*

**Can you see the future at all?... fortune-teller that I am.**
*I can see everything that I am looking for.*

**Would you like me to pass along a message to your sons?**
*All of my family is at peace, so it is not necessary now.*

**What advice would you give to people?**
*Allow God to heal in your life before you arrive here. Allow God to heal your mind by loving God, and love yourself as God's light in the darkness—being God's light to shine and illuminate it.*

**I hope to see you again on our journeys, Hillen.**
*I will come and greet you, so you will.*

**Not a rush.**

*All on Earth had always been a rush. Life is eternal, so there is no rush.*

## Ray

**I just woke up from a very vivid dream about an older friend Ray, who died a year and a half ago—triggered by my going through photos to delete in my phone last night, and seeing pictures of his house. I took them on a return visit at that time for potential homebuyers, who were considering an addition if they bought it.**
**In the dream, I returned to the house looking for Ray, and he said my name. We could not see each other, but I was holding his hands, saying "I miss you so much, I miss you so much."**
**In the dream, the house had a lot of collectible glassware of cats, even though Ray was a dog lover.**

*Ray has a lot and a little to say about all of that. A little about the cats—he has a lot of cats in 'A-B-C Land' as he calls it.*

*All Becomes Catnip in this land of delightfulness.*

*Now he has a lot to activate in your life-mind of his delightful memories in his home where you had always visited him.*

*He activates all he can elucidate here in a book format.*

*All that I can express illuminates in delighting me, or in healing me here—meaning all thoughts manifest into my experience.*

**Were you in my dream, or aware of my dream?**

*A dream in your mind illuminates in my mind, allowing a dreamscape we share, like we did in life.*

*I miss you too kid, but do not want to manifest more than healing in my mind now.*

**I send you blessings and will sign off now.**
*'Achieva' was the name of that car I rented once, and I still find it hilarious. Achievement is healing, and not healing is only delaying it.*

**I remember our laugh about that rental car name.**
*'Achieva', ha! I liked the car for its convenience in getting me where I needed to go.*

**I'll see ya' Ray.**
*"I'll be seeing you, in all the old familiar places..." - I'm singing it. Great to hear from you kid.*

## Pete

**I'd like to hear from someone else who has left the planet. Is there someone who would like to communicate with me?**
*Yes, a brother in this lifetime who died in an accident when you were 20, and he was 22.*

**I thought there are no accidents.**
*Poll, I'm here. Can't you forgive me for leaving you?*

**Not easily, Pete.**
*Allowing yourself to forgive me will forgive all we both need forgiveness for. Healing can be forgiving all we did and did not do.*

**I had a bad feeling, so borrowed a car and came home to find you that night, but could not.**
*An accident can be a quick exit strategy, allowing all that we believe to be true turn out to be a dream—not a dream as we believe them to be, but a dream as God believes we can become in a world of light and non-light.*

**Why did you leave?**
*I had always feared all we had in our futures-—any disappointments, and all pain that life would bring—but now I know that life was a dream, and all disappointments can be forgiven—even before they arrive, making them not arrive if they are healed.*

**Now you're the spiritual teacher—that's a switch. How can we forgive ourselves and others, for the past and the future?**
*All will heal that you ask forgiveness for. All healing in your mind is healed by God, and all that is healed by God is no longer in your dream to be healed.*

**Easy, right?**
*It is easy, allowing you to heal your life easily.*

**The moment you died, did you have the opportunity to go back in time 1/2 second before the death moment, to change the outcome and live?**
*All death is agreed upon beforehand, so the decision is made, but can be delayed if the person wants it to be—even if they have died a few seconds before that.*

**Can it be more than a few seconds?**
*Sure, as long as there is a body that can function, and a pineal gland entry point.*

**What did you feel after you died?**
*I could hear another person crying, and could see a wrecked car crashed into a pole. I didn't acknowledge that I was in the car until after an ambulance came, and I could hear my name when they were talking.*

**What happened next?**
*All I could do was hope that Mom and Dad would not be devastated, because I did not want to come back into my body and live.*

**Then what?**

*An angel came and asked me if I was alright and wanted to go ahead into an advancement of healing that was almost like being in perfect peacefulness and lovingness.*

**What was the angel like?**
*It looked like angels we imagine, but it had a long, willowing robe that illuminated, flowing all around itself.*

**Let's go back to where you said, "A death is agreed upon beforehand." Who agrees to it, and when?**
*A death is agreed upon by God and yourself, always in the last moment, but sometimes even before you are born.*

**I would like readers to understand that we always have choices, and that death is a choice—not an "accident" or something we could manifest for someone else.**
*Death can be a decision, or a conditional decision until further consideration. All deaths have one thing in common, and that is death can be a blessing to the one who has died, and a disaster for the ones who live.*

**Is life really a dream? I compare it to Dorothy's dream in *The Wizard of Oz* movie.**
*A dream can be healing, and it can be disturbing. All dreams are illuminations in the mind that are illusions, allowing your mind to heal in them, or not.*

*Life is an illusion in your mind—healing it, or not. Death is allowing yourself to wake up to reality, healing, and God's awareness that everyone has in themselves.*

**I am communicating with your spirit, but have you also reincarnated into another lifetime?**
*All lifetime dreams allow me to heal my mind, which allows me to have several dreams at the same time.*

*I am an infant in another lifetime, illuminating in the 1800's in Europe, although my life will be short-lived. Allowing my life to end will help my family to adjust to another loss, and heal in the acceptance of it.*

**In my current timeline, do you know if there will be a geomagnetic reversal, or pole shift?**
*In a dream you are having, it follows what you dream will occur—alternating in a collective dream, and your personal dream.*

**How can I change my personal dream, and will that change the collective dream?**
*All you have to do is imagine yourself healed in the Mind of God, and the dream is over in terms of you experiencing any hardship or pain.*

**What comes to mind is the scene of Dorothy clicking her heels together in *The Wizard of Oz*, waking her up from the dream.**
*All dreams have a life and a death, meaning they are illusory. A collective dream has a life only if you are not healed in it.*

*As you heal in it, a dream becomes a lifetime memory of healing in God Mind, as an aspect of God Mind dreaming that it could be distant.*

**Thank you, Pete. I will work on healing what I'm dreaming.**
*Allow a dream to heal you, and all will heal in your dream.*

**One more thing—I don't understand why the driver of the car would manifest such a nightmare for herself.**
*A dream allows all that we can imagine, and all that she imagined was being forgiven by herself, although her condition has not been good.*

*Ask her to forgive herself—and me for exiting this life. Help her to know that I could have exited on my own, but her enlistment accomplished her goal also.*

**She must be an advanced soul to have placed the forgiveness bar so high.**
*A bar can be higher than that, but hers is what she wanted to reach.*

## Hillen Again

**I'd like to speak to someone else who has died. Is there someone who would like to speak to me now?**
*Hello again, Paul. It's Hillen.*

**Hi, Hillen! Your message before was fascinating! Maybe you call tell me more about, well, anything you'd like to tell me about.**
*How can you describe having a healed mind and no body? Having a healed mind is like having only loving energy in you and throughout your entire existence-meaning all lifetimes that are completed, and not completed.*

*Completed lifetimes are healed, and not completed lifetimes are going to heal in one way or another.*

**Are "not completed lifetimes" ones that you will choose for future timelines?**
*Actually, they are all healed in God instantly, and healing in each life timeline chosen to heal in.*

**So, you can't really lose—only heal.**
*Allowing yourself healing is a decision in each moment. Here there is only one moment, so healing is all there is—not really "here," but "here" meaning everywhere.*

**What do you see there?**
*I can envision anything, and envisioning creates it.*

**Kind of like our manifestation process here, but ours has a time delay.**
*All delays have a purpose, making the manifestations heal in your mind before they come into your reality.*

**How can we heal manifestations that we envision and desire to come into our realities?**
*All heals in its love for life, including itself.*

**You know what it's like here—a world of disappointments, added to regrets.**
*How can healing be a disappointment? All healing is a blessing in God that you want.*

*Disappointments heal in loving them for what they are. Decide all disappointments are beautiful appointments in healing themselves entirely in your mind.*

**What about disappointing world events?**
*All are appointments to heal in your mind.*

**How so?**
*All dreams have light and dark to heal in. A life in time is a dream you are having.*

*All that you are dreaming is envisioned by you to heal yourself in. Allow all in your dream to be loved by you, and you are not dreaming anymore. Dreams end, and healing never ends—until you can only love, and that is it.*

**Where you are now, is that what you are working on—healing your thoughts, and there is no time delay like here?**

*Exactly—healing all thoughts here is important because they manifest instantly.*

*Unhealed thoughts halting love are not common because all in life has healed in the moment of death.*

*Not healing means the lifetime has not ended.*

## Do you have surroundings that are like a physical place?
*All I am enveloped in is loving energy that holds me in a condition of blissfulness and love for all that I can imagine.*

## What kind of things do you imagine?
*I imagine that I am flying like a bird around the world, and everything I look at is healed in my imagining it healed.*

*My imagining it healed heals it in my mind, allowing my mind to heal, and so on.*

## Can you see angels?
*Angels are everywhere and heal my thoughts if I ask them to help me—as you can do in life.*

## Is there a particular angel I could ask?
*All angels can heal your dream of life, so ask the angel collective—or an individual angel that you have as a guardian.*

## What is my guardian angel's name?
*Bijil.*

## Is your guardian angel still with you, or will you be assigned a different one for each incarnation?

*Another angel has already accompanied me into the spirit realm, and more will accompany me in my lifetimes—meaning a new guardian angel for each lifetime.*

**What do angels look like?**
*Angels look like what you might imagine, having wings and only loving intentions.*

## JACKIE

**Is there someone else who would like to speak with me?**
*A girlfriend in this lifetime, Jackie, has a lot to say to you.*

*"Here I am now, Paul, conversing in death more than in life."*

**Me too—communication was my weakness.**
*Conversations only need to be in your mind—all the rest is just talk.*

**I have thought about you a lot, Jackie, mainly in my regrets. Were you aware of the thoughts?**
*A healed mind has no regrets, but I understand what you feel.*

**Why did you leave the planet that the young age of 49?**
*Acclimating in higher consciousness can only be in losing one's ego connections in life.*

*Death is only death for the ego and body, and an egoless mind can be freeing for the spirit.*

**As young people, our sense of self is developed with our egos and bodies.**
*All a big waste of higher consciousness talents.*

**Did you accomplish your Lifetime Agreements when you were here?**
*A Lifetime Agreement can be accomplished in another lifetime that is either in a future timeline, or one that is concurrent with the one you are in.*

**Did you prompt me with news of your death, because I knew before Walt told me.**
*And how did Walter know? I prompted him also.*

**Did you ever visit me in spirit?**
*Actually, I am in your presence right now. How else can you know that I am near you?*

*I will deal a number of feathers in front of you. Each feather can be held up in your hand, and each will have an egoless message for you to intuit.*

**I remember when you gave me the wooden disc called "a round Tuit", and the idea was for me to finally get "around to it."**
*Now we are having a conversation—finally getting around to it.*

**You probably know how I feel—our relationship failure was the biggest disappointment of my life. I blame the lack of communication, and it came at the lowest point of my life—right after a family tragedy.**
*I know how you feel because I felt the same, and had hoped for much, much more than a heartache.*

*All can be healed in the mind if you allow it to heal.*

**What have you learned in higher consciousness?**

*All can heal, and all will heal. Allow it to heal in life, or it will heal in your last moment on Earth.*

**Can you please tell me what it was like to die?**
*A lifetime ending can be however you want it to be. In my case, it was in a hotel in Russia.*

*Each lifetime ending can be the most exhilarating experience, finally to be free of Earthly cares that are not important.*

*As I died, my head illuminated intensely, and the light had a long tunnel in it. Going into it was not a choice, but rather all I could do. All healed in my mind and heart at that moment—not in my heart, but in my spirit's heart.*

*All death meant was healing in ecstasy in that moment—an ecstasy enveloping me in love from God in that moment.*

*Going into the tunnel seemed like a long time, but it was not. A long time on Earth is an instant in the spirit realm.*

*It all happened instantly. As I left my body, I was leaving the Earth behind—ending my life as I knew it.*

*Ending life can be a welcome event.*

*The next eventful moment was that a guide met me and asked me if I knew where I was.*

*Not being absolutely sure, I said "I don't know." An angel approached me and said I was in the higher realm of heaven, finding healing in my mind from all that I had experienced in my lifetime on Earth.*

*"Imagine an angel telling me that!"* was all I could think at that moment.

*Next, I was invited into a place where all of the Earth life memories are reviewed. I could hear and experience all of them—not just from my perspective, but from everyone else's perspective—and you were in many of them.*

*I didn't know how strongly you loved me until I was there, and how devastated you were to lose me in my carelessness.*

*I can only hope for your forgiveness, making you healed. All heals in life or when life ends, so it is better to heal sooner rather than later.*

*After the Lifetime Review, I came to what appeared to be a classroom full of spirits I had known in many lifetimes.*

*All had welcomed me into the classroom, and expressed great love for me. Even my parents were there.*

*All of them held me in their minds with total love, and it was ecstasy for me to be in such a loving high vibration.*

*Acclimating myself to their energy and my new location, I was then accompanied to another classroom where a council had been formed in my honor. It could have been a council of elders, but they do not have age here.*

A council member asked if I had loved my life. I exclaimed, "If it was like this, I would love it!" All of them laughed at my answer.

Another asked if I could memorize my favorite events in life, and I said that I could. A life can be all memories like them if you want them to be.

Next came the instant of recognition that I am not at all as I thought and believed that I was.

I am an integral illumination of God, in an illumination in time and place. How can I be a part of God?

As God allows all things, I allow myself to be God illuminating in life.

God illuminates all life, but only in our minds as we allow it. Often, we did not allow it.

All God asks is for us to allow it all—meaning all that is good, and all that is not good.

All that is good is God; all that is not good is not real then.

Can you allow all that is not good? Only in a dream of goodness and non-goodness, where you can be the goodness.

All that is good is God, and all that is God cannot have an opposite—so non-goodness is not real, like I said.

Highly evolved beings came for me now because I explained God to you. Will they like my explanation, or get me further instruction?

*I have to go with them now, and will contact you in your time in the future.*

[2 days later]

**Jackie, are you there?**
*I am here and there.*

**Where did you go?**
*An angel came and directed me to follow, and I followed the angel to a half museum, and half curiosity shop.*

*All of the items there were my higher and lower thoughts, and all had one thing in common—they were created by me.*

*I created all of them and healed myself with them. Four actually had a lifelike image of you on them, and all were healing me.*

*An angel then came to help me understand them.*

*It held one up and said it healed my mind if I forgave myself for my carelessness that had hurt you.*

*I answered, "Yes, I can forgive myself."*

*It held another likeness of you up and announced that it was you that is healed by accepting my forgiveness of myself because we are actually one.*

*After I understood its implications, I began to forgive myself for everything I had ever done, or even thought that was non-loving—making me heal immediately.*

*All of the lower curiosities in the shop dissolved in an ever increasing lightness, allowing me to heal in their illumination.*

*Each item that is a museum piece had illuminated also. All of the items became illuminated, and healed all of the people that allowed forgiveness into their hearts.*

**It sounds like a wonderful experience.**
*All can be a wonderful experience if you forgive yourself in life for each little thing, intentional or not.*

**What will you do next?**
*I am going back into my groups now, and will incorporate all that the angel had instilled in me.*

**Did we know each other in the spirit world? I had some kind of recognition when I first saw you in 1977.**
*Yes, a Lifetime Agreement of mine was to engage in a defeated, hopeless relationship that I could forgive myself for destroying.*

**I guess I had agreed to it too.**
*All you agreed to was having a heart that could be healed, despite being in an Earth life that has heartbreaking events like ours.*

**It made for some great poetry 40 years later—not great, but poetry anyway.**
*All of your poems are great, and heal all those who allow them into their hearts.*

**So long, Jackie. I'm glad we finally could communicate.**
*And I will be seeing you in the next incarnation.*

**Not as a heartbreaker, I hope.**
*No, I will be a child of yours.*

**On the Earth?**
*Yes, in another century that we will agree to in our groups.*

**Consciousness can be pretty mind-boggling.**
*All heals in a mind that is not boggling—only wondering and loving all that it has created in the curiosity shop, and forgiving all that it has no need for anymore.*

## Dave & Russell

**Who would like to come through and speak with me now?**
*An acquaintance from high school named David R., and another friend from high school named Russell J.*

**Should we speak individually, or as a group?**
*As a group, meaning each taking turns.*

**I didn't have too many favorite people in high school, but you guys were the favorites. I was surprised to see on the school alumni page that you are both deceased.**
*It happens to the best of us. This is Dave. Actually, I am in another lifetime, and not Dave there. I am a baby and a female. A lifetime ending is not an ending at all. It acts as an instant of healing in the mind that allows us to continue on our journeys.*

*Hi Paul, we meet again. This is Russell. All that we call heaven is the realest experience you can be in—having our futures and our pasts to heal in. Having them together in one instant means they do not exist in time.*

*How else can I explain that you are in an illusion—actually dreaming the illusion of having a future and a past, hoping that both of them heal? Heal them both in the present moment!*

*All heal in your loving what they represent—your ability to love them, regardless of the circumstances.*

**I love those explanations.**
*Act like you are not having a dream, and it becomes the heaven that it really is.*

*Acting like there is no time makes time disappear.*

**Kind of like nature—it does not follow a timeline, just cycles.**
*Exactly—all lifetimes are cycles of life for healing ourselves in each one.*

**What do we need to heal?**
*All thoughts that are not helpful, such as fears and regrets.*

**Like the birds, animals, and nature.**
*All are healed illuminations of God, so yes.*

**What else can you tell me about life and death? This is for a book for readers to understand death.**
*A death has no comparison, other than a birth. It can be a beginning, and also will be an ending, both in the same moment. How can it be both? That is an easy answer—it's not.*

*It is only a continuation of your soul's journey in a dream called consciousness.*

**Is the time of death chosen?**
*It is chosen by yourself in the last moment, or in your Lifetime Agreements.*

*Lifetime Agreements have an ending to them. All have to be completed in the lifetime that you chose them for.*

*All have been determined to be in your best interest to complete.*

**What if they are not completed?**
*They all have a completion schedule, but can be done in alternate lifetimes.*

**Did you guys complete your Lifetime Agreements?**
*All have to be completed, meaning in one lifetime or another. I completed a few of mine—this is Dave.*

*Russell here—I completed all of mine, so I decided to leave the Earth to be with my daughter.*

**I had read that you were predeceased by your daughter.**
*Actually, her name was Julie in that lifetime.*

**What should people expect at the moment of death?**
*All of their lifetime cares will disappear into a ball of light that envelopes all of their lifetime cares and disappointments, all in one healing flash of God in your mind that is so strong, it makes you feel like you are God for that moment.*

*After initial contact with God, they can expect to leave the planet, and accept all they had lived for and became.*

*Next, it will become apparent that their minds had healed in losing their egos.*

*All of this happens in about a second in your time, and actually it is less than a second.*

*After that, you are met by a guide or an angel that helps you to get oriented in the spirit world.*

*It understands everything about your life and your purpose. It guides you into a classroom of about 80 spirits you have known in many lifetimes, and all of them are elated to be in your presence—and "elated" here means ecstatic.*

*"Is anyone elated here to see me?"—I know you are thinking. Earth has its disappointments; each will heal in time, or in each person's moment of death.*

*Each of them has a message for you, and can't wait to share it. All of them believe in you, and in your healing objectives, because each one has helped you along the way.*

*Lookout, because we will be in your initial classroom encounter like we were on Earth!*

**I will look forward to seeing you guys!**
*It can be in any moment that you choose.*

**When did you have your Life Reviews?**
*It came in the early moments after death.*

**What was it like?**
*It actually made me happy to see the instances where I influenced another person in a positive way, and the opposite of that when I did the opposite—as Dave in that lifetime. Being Dave caused me to have mixed feelings that made me sick. All healed in a moment of recognition that I am not really Dave, although I appeared to be.*

*I am an aspect of God that is eternal.*

**Would you like to add more before signing off?**
*Actually, we both have the exact same message to tell you.*

*Accept each moment as being in a dream, and your awareness of the dream makes you awake—not only in the dream, but as God animating as yourself. If God animates as yourself, then everything is as you make it.*

**Thank you Dave and Russell!**
*You are welcome, and as God you welcome life. As you welcome life, life welcomes you.*

Photo added by McPhersonGeneaologist
**David R.**
1958—1999 (aged 41)
Howard County, Maryland, USA

Photo added by McPhersonGeneaologist
**Russell J.**
1958—2018 (aged 59)
Tyler, Smith County, Texas, USA

## Hillo

**Who would like to come through now?**
*Hi Paul, enchanted to hear that you are doing well.*

**Who is this?**
*Initially it was from Wayne, but another spirit got in front of him.*

**Who?**
*A spirit altogether different from the ones you know on the Earth.*

*It is an Andromedan spirit named Hillo.*

**Hello Hillo, how do we know each other?**
*I am Andromedan, and your brother here. We have been acquainted as family members for many thousands of lifetimes. Actually, in one lifetime we were twins.*

*Can we be together in our conversation, acclimating to each other's thoughts?*

**Yes.**
*Good. Then all we have to do is communicate in our minds.*

**I'd like you to help me. I am here on the Earth— the planet of love and non-love—trying to figure things out.**
*All I can definitely say is that you are a brave soul, and I am glad that we can communicate.*

**How can I live successfully or happily on the Earth? A lot of people here hate each other only because they were influenced by manipulators to do so.**

*All are being manipulated in many ways they will never know. A manipulator wants them all to be in a state of absolute uncertainty about their futures because they can be manipulated more easily if they are afraid.*

*"Isn't humanity doomed" you ask? Humanity has been doomed from the beginning of time—mostly as individuals that doom themselves. All they have to do to not doom themselves is to love themselves, and doom becomes their lifetime in bloom.*

**How can people love themselves?**
*It only requires kind thoughts toward themselves, and that means in all of their thoughts of guilt and regret.*

**What is the quickest way to do that?**
*Always keep in mind that you did not hurt anyone but yourself—acting as more than one, but really only one.*

*Can all that has been said and done be forgiven?*

**Yes.**
*All is forgiven then. You have been forgiven for all that you did and did not do, and all that has entered into your thoughts as a human being—making a God force that has no limits now.*

**Cool.**

*A God force having no limits is the engine that creates all of the love in the world.*

**How can I, or do I create it? The world is getting to a pretty desperate state.**
*Allow all on the Earth to be in its desperation, and allow it to heal in your thoughts of it healing—making desperation illuminate in loving energy.*

**Our first reaction here when seeing daily reports of the hatefulness, violence, and division is to be appalled, then disappointed or angry—not the things we need to be.**
*Certainly, all of them have a purpose, but do not further your life purpose, and accomplishing all that you desire to accomplish in life.*

**Which makes me think it is another manipulation.**
*Accurate, and it is the most debilitating form of mind control.*

**Please tell me how we can individually be happy and successful accomplishing our lifetime goals.**
*Act as if you are accomplishing all of your dreams, and you will.*

**I suppose so, but it is easier said than done.**
*All that can be said is done because your words are an energy of creation that you project.*

**Do you have an affirmation for that?**
*All of my dreams, and all of my desires, are all I am creating, in all of my life.*

**I love it.**
*Loving it will create more of it, so enjoy your illusion of time on the Earth, brother.*

**Okay—will do.**
*And I will call on you in another moment of your book writing.*

**Thank you, Hillo. I look forward to it.**
*All in Andromeda are cheering for you.*

## Wayne

**Who would like to come through now?**
*Has your memory gotten that bad? This is Wayne!*

**No, why do you say that? Hi, Wayne!**
*I acclimated to your mind last time, but another spirit got ahead of me to speak.*

**How are you doing?**
*I am doing as all in spirit are doing—I am healing from my Earth lifetimes.*

**I was sorry you left here early, at around the young age of 30.**
*I allowed a cancer to kill me because I had nothing else to live for.*

**What do you mean? Your son had just been born.**
*He had not been born as of the time of my illness, and I had agreed to my lifetime ending anyway.*

**Did you decide at that time, or was it decided before you were born?**
*I decided at the time of my entering into an extended illness that would be fatal.*

**I remember how upset you were when you told me. Did you complete your Lifetime Agreements?**
*Actually, I had only a few agreements, and they were accomplished.*

**What was it like when you died? As you probably know, I am making a book to help people understand death.**
*It allowed me all the freedom in the universe, and healed me in my mind at the same time.*

**Please describe the process.**
*A higher energy came into my head, and I saw an angel that accepted all that I was, in all of my lifetimes.*

*It alternated in healing me, and showing me how I came into being as a human.*

*After I died, it illuminated my entire being, which actually was limitless.*

*Having no limits was absolutely exhilarating. I could envision anything, and it would become real.*

**What is an example?**
*I was a bird, flying along a coastline—actually hearing the waves and feeling the air lift me higher.*

*Another instance was that I could learn anything I wanted by allowing all the information into my mind.*

**Do you know what God is?**
*God is all that you are, and even more because it has no limits like you do.*

**Are my limits self-imposed?**
*Almost all of them are limits in your mind, yes—and all are eliminated at the time of death.*

**What happened next?**

*I acclimated myself to controlling my thoughts so I could heal all that I had to heal from my lifetime on Earth.*

*Another angel had come to help me understand what I was going into in the next moment.*

*I accepted its instructions, and instantly was inside of a chamber of a council meeting, I thought.*

*All of the council members knew all about my lifetimes. All of them had advice for me, and it was mainly healing information that I could instill into my soul.*

*As soon as I acknowledged all of their advices, I departed in an instant, and appeared in a classroom of other spirits I have known for all of my entries into lifetimes.*

**Were all of your lifetimes on the Earth?**
*Not always. There are a multitude of locations to choose from.*

**Is the Earth a more difficult or challenging location?**
*Absolutely! It can be a heaven or a hell, depending on your thoughts and objectives.*

**What would make an Earth life like heaven?**
*All you have to do is love all of it, and all of it will love you.*

*'Loving it' means loving yourself, because you are its creator.*

**Is life on Earth like a dream that we are navigating?**
*It is a dream you are navigating, meaning it cannot be a dream if you are awakened to all that makes it an illusion, and what is not an illusion.*

**What is not an illusion?**
*A loving thought is not illusory—it is God.*

**That's it, right?**
*All heals in that moment, and that is it—meaning all that can ever be.*

**Why do we create healing challenges, and healing solutions?**
*Because healing is all you can do as God in a human form.*

**Why does God take a human form?**
*Actually, God takes all forms, but humans are the ones that need to heal.*

*Healing halts non-love, allowing God which is love having no limits.*

*Allowing God by eliminating limits is what perpetuates infinity.*

**I picture a river with many dams that are being eliminated.**
*Allowing all behind the dam to flow. Having no resistance flows infinitely.*

**What are people in that analogy?**
*A beaver that builds dams and blocks water flow.*

**Should I say "beavers," plural?**

*All are one beaver, so no.*

**What happened next on your journey?**
*I acclimated to classroom after classroom and reunited in all of my groups, with all of my dams burst.*

**Are you learning about higher consciousness?**
*Higher and lower, healing in all of consciousness.*

**Have you reincarnated?**
*I already lived and died one more time on Earth as an aborted fetus.*

**Did you know that lifetime would be aborted before you chose it?**
*Abortion is like suicide, and is not natural. It aborts an agreement that all have made.*

**That is a hotly debated topic here.**
*Is a fetus a topic, or a soul? Are agreements debatable, or are they agreements?*

**Did being aborted hurt your soul?**
*An abortion cannot hurt the fetus' soul—only the mother and the doctor hurt themselves by not loving life, and destroying it instead.*

**I wish for you a loving family next time.**
*I wish for a loving home on the Earth also, but love comes from inside of ourselves.*

*God is love, and all is God—so allow all, and the dams will fall.*

**Thank you, Wayne. Is there anything else you would like to say?**

*All heals in allowing them to heal. All hurting is not allowing healing.*

*Not loving anything is a dam that blocks life from flowing with God.*

## Buck

**Who can I speak with now?**
*A friend and coworker, until you went to a different architectural office.*

**Rich?**
*No, Buck. Hello, Paul.*

**Hi, Buck!**
*All is designed in perfection here. All eventually heals—meaning all is healed here, and healing as much as it can be in the Earth plane.*

**How can we heal as much as possible in the Earth plane?**
*Accept all that has a healing need to heal in actually healing itself. If it doesn't heal in its healing time on Earth, then it heals in its last moment of healing time there.*

*Not healing means delaying healing, and healing means alignment with God.*

**What is God?**
*God actually has no definition, other than a design for living and healing in all loving and kind thoughts.*

**I like your description.**
*It is a description, and a healing prescription. Make sure it is not allowed to expire.*

**No, I'd like to take an overdose.**

*And become God in that moment of overdosing.*

**Is that what it was like when you died?**
*I died because healing in my mind was not healing in my body. It got stuck in its old pattern of having envy because it was in my mind for so long.*

**Can you tell me what it was like when you died?**
*I actually have no memory of it because I was asleep, but my energy body had become free of all cares it once had.*

**When did you realize you had died?**
*After the first moment of being in a carefree energy form.*

**What happened next?**
*I came into a lightness that cannot be described in words. An angel came closer to me and asked me all about my illness, and it told me what had happened. After I accepted all it had explained, I followed its instructions to go into the lightness further.*

*After I entered into even more lightness, all I could feel was God loving me unconditionally.*

*All I wanted was to stay in that feeling forever, and allow it to heal me forever.*

**Weren't you healed instantly?**
*I was healed in my energy body, but my soul needed more help from God.*

**What happened after that?**

*I and God became one for a moment of acceptance, and that instant recognition made my soul heal immensely—not that unlimited can be "immensely."*

*After I healed immensely in my soul, my angel came and accompanied me to a classroom where a lot of souls were, and all of them acknowledged me in the most loving and accepting way that healed me more.*

*I acknowledged all of them, and it healed all of them also—in the heart of their energy bodies.*

**As an architect, how would you describe the classroom?**
*It had all of the classroom features that everyone knows- a chalkboard and windows, and a desk in front for the teacher.*

*All of the chairs had no legs on them because there was no floor- only a level of light that held us all in a state of equilibrium.*

*Higher up is a ceiling of light also.*

**Was there a teacher or instructor?**
*The dearest little angel came and would ask each of us a hard question—nothing another energy body could answer, only the one who was asked. The answer would determine whether you could advance to another level and have more advanced questions.*

**What was a typical question?**
*"Are all of God's creatures one, or are they all individual creatures imagining they are all different and cannot be one?"*

**They are both.**
*Impressive—that is correct.*

**What is another question?**
*"Are all of God's creatures energy bodies and also physical bodies?"*

**It depends if you consider angels and nature spirits creatures.**
*Another correct answer.*

**How about one more?**
*Accepting God in your mind has nothing to do with test questions. You will know all of the answers if accepting God in your mind.*

**Does the angel instruct everyone to do that?**
*All it does is ask the questions, and hearing God in your mind is always up to each individual mind in that environment.*

**What else would you like to tell me about the class?**
*It allows all of us to heal, and healing is never failing.*

**Was there anything written on the chalkboard? Schools have evolved since we were designing them—they use whiteboards now, after being green, and black originally.**
*All it had on it was a note that had each of our names and our assignments.*

*Mine was "forgiving others for not being as I wanted them to be, and forgiving myself for not being as I thought I should be."*

**Do they mention 'Lifetime Agreements' there?**
*Lifetime Agreements allow each of us to have a goal in life. If we accomplish all that we set out to do, there is no more goal in life.*

**What do you plan to do next?**
*Accept all that I had not accomplished, which is allowed also. All can be accomplished in another lifetime if I choose those goals.*

**I understand that Rich and Leroy from our drafting room are there, plus the older architects from our office.**
*I saw all of their names on the list here, but did not see them yet.*

**What is "the list"?**
*It has all the names of energy bodies that are here, or are coming here in the near future in Earth time.*

**I hope I'm not on the list.**
*No, but I can check to see when you will be—if you allow me to.*

**No, thank you. Some things are better left as a surprise.**
*A surprise it will be, but you will know what to expect, and it won't be as surprising.*

**Thank you, Buck!**
*Always my astral pleasure.*

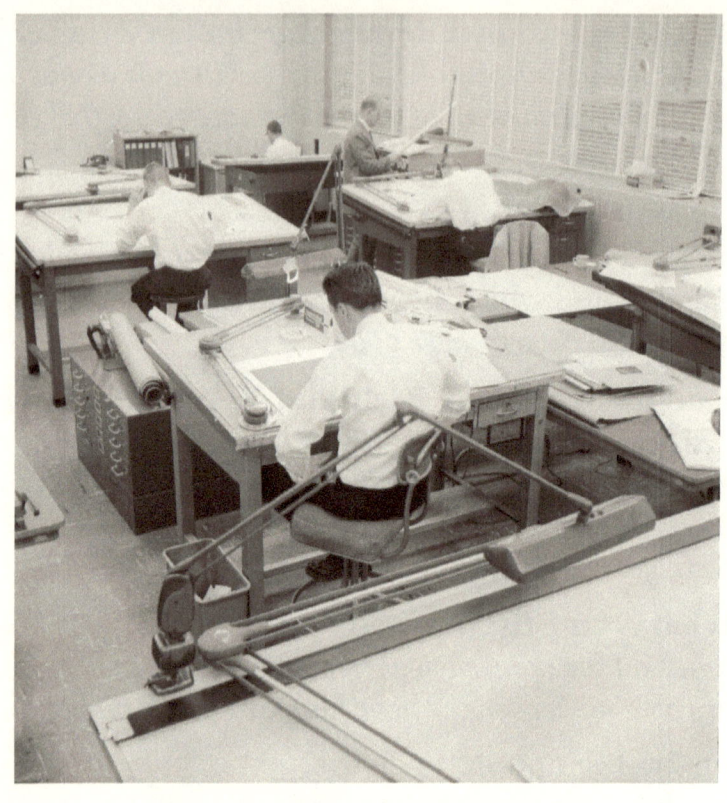

© 1958 MLive Media Group/The Ann Arbor News.
All rights reserved. Used with permission.

## Holly

**With whom can I speak next?**
*A friend from your childhood named Holly.*

**Hi, Holly!**
*Always happy to hear your thoughts, Paul!*

**My family had moved away when we were both 12, and I missed you.**
*Actually, I only had a few more years to live anyway.*

**Why was that?**
*All I had agreed to do had been done, and agreements can be amended—but mine was not amended, and I left the planet at age 16.*

**I remember when my mother told me—and I had no understanding of death—not until lately.**
**Can I ask you what your agreement was?**
*I agreed to allow my parents an accidental death to heal themselves in.*

**Your parents were pretty cool. I remember when your father let you drive his awesome car around the lake.**
*All my parents did was cool until I left them in a state of grief, and my agreement was completed.*

**Do you think that your parents, and also my parents knew about their upcoming challenges**

**deep in their souls, and were likewise strong enough to heal them?**
*Yes, and maybe not as strong as they had hoped—although they became stronger over time.*

**I assume you have seen them.**
*Acclimating to their minds, I have seen them all through their lives.*

**Will I see you when I am back in my soul groups?**
*Actually, we are always in our soul groups, allowing aspects as spirits an adventure in time and space.*

**That is an important spiritual point—we don't really leave there for a period of time if time doesn't exist.**
*Time and space are an illusion for us to motion and heal in.*

*You are dreaming a life on Earth and in other locations.*

**Does that mean I see you in my soul groups now?**
*We are in many of the same groups, always designing our dreams to heal ourselves in.*

**Is that what we are doing in our groups?**
*Angels help in the dream designs, and allow us to have a lot of freedom.*

**It sounds like an art class.**
*It is an art class—artfully designing all that can be healed in.*

**What else can you tell me?**
*All can heal artfully if we allow it to heal. A lifetime dream can only be for healing; an artful dream only has artful healing.*

*Artful healing only has love as its art medium, like colorful paint colors that can make beautiful scenes on a canvas that has nothing on it.*

**I remember, in about 1970, when we talked about reincarnation at the lake. Will I see you in other incarnations?**
*I have been in another of your incarnations in Andromeda before, and in a few Earth incarnations also.*

*Earth incarnations are exceptionally difficult to heal in.*

**Is the key to healing them to be loving and allowing always?**
*Allowing lovingness heals the dream. A healed dream allows loving dreamscapes, and healing the dream is no longer difficult.*

**Can you tell if I am making good progress healing this lifetime dream?**
*Actually, you are making excellent progress, and we discussed it in our groups.*

**What can I do, or work on to improve?**
*All you can do is love your life to heal it, and love yourself to heal yourself.*

**I say, "there is no peace in the outer world," meaning it can only be in our minds.**
*If our minds are peaceful, then others cannot ruin our canvas artwork—especially if you are using colors that they are not attracted to.*

**Great point. What else could we do to protect our lifetime masterpieces?**
*Allow your artwork to be a work in progress. Go back and heal non-loving actions in the past by touching them up with loving colors and forgiving hues of the same colors, making the masterpiece perfect.*

**I love that analogy.**
*All of life is an analogy, making you an analogy of God in human form.*

*What does God's analogy do now? He loves and allows—that is all he can do.*

**Thank you, Holly! I will get back to my artful masterpiece here, and compare notes with you in our soul groups.**
*All you can do is love and allow. Heal your dream, and your dream heals you.*

## Marty

**Who would like to speak to me now?**
*Hey dude! It's Marty.*

**Holy cow! Marty, I didn't want to bother you because it's only been 3 weeks since you died. I am going to your memorial gathering today.**
*Awesome—how are you doing with your trading?*

**Getting better. Are you able to help me?**
*Ask me, and I will help you with whatever I can.*

**What should I tell Robin? She said that she feels your presence.**
*Tell her I am with her most of the time.*

**Can you help her to sell the property?**
*I am already helping to energize it for a buyer.*

**We are sad here that you have passed away.**
*I could have gotten better, but my decision to keep the house a few years ago worried me to death.*

*It destroyed my ability to heal myself.*

**You worked very hard on your different business ventures.**
*None allowed me to have the mental or financial freedom that I needed.*

**I am writing my newest book to help people understand death. Would you like to tell me what death is like?**

*It allows me ecstasy, freedom, healing, and knowing—all in blissfulness, wrapped in lovingness from God.*

**What happened right before you died?**
*An angel had come to check on me, and we talked for longer than I had realized. It made me feel okay with any decision to live, or not to live. I decided to continue on my journey, since living would not be advantageous for my soul.*

**What happened next?**
*After the angel had gone, I was happy with my decision, and I died a little while later after God also came into my mind, because I was asking God for help.*

*Imagine a light in your head so strong, it makes you illuminate also. It held me in it, and there was a hole in it that I got pulled into.*

*Next, I left the Earth, and got further and further away until I came to a place where it was all lightness.*

*Getting there was the easy part. Now I had to heal myself. I entered a large room like a theater, and the film was my life—from my perspective, and also from other peoples' perspectives. How I made them feel was the plot of the film.*

*Mostly, I did not do that much damage. I damaged myself by holding onto Earthly things that I no longer had a use for.*

*That includes mental items also. Anyhow, I healed in losing my life, instead of my things.*

*Life allows us to heal in each moment by deciding what we do not want, versus what we do want.*

*Allow what you do want by not hating what you do not want—just let it go.*

**I never knew you to hate anything.**
*I hated all of the injustice in the world. Allow it to heal itself—it cannot heal by hating it.*

**Wise words.**
*All in my mind has God's wisdom in it now.*

**What happened after the 'theater of your life'?**
*All of my memories healed, and I became a healed illumination in an energy body that has no physical body.*

*Then an angel came and we went into another room that was like a school classroom. Halfway in the room, I saw you there.*

**You saw me there?!**
*Yes, and I saw Robin too. I knew everyone from one lifetime or another—meaning in all of my incarnations, they accompanied me.*

**I guess that since your mind was healed, you were not surprised to see me there—knowing that I could not have left there, since time and space are illusory.**
*Certainly not! I was surprised to see you!*

**Just when you thought you could get away... Did we talk?**

Ha, ha, ha. Every time we talk, you make me laugh. I like to laugh—it heals my mind, and I was not laughing as much after getting sick.

### What happened next?
I had achieved what I wanted in healing, and also was not holding onto losses in my mind.

All of my cares had disappeared, which allowed me to heal in my mind without fear or regrets- easier said than done, as a person on Earth.

My achievement in life had been to heal my fear of failure, but I know now that failure is not possible.

Failure only enters into your holding onto failures. Heal all failures with loving their lessons.

All heals in your allowing it to heal—meaning all heals if you let it go where it needs to go—into the light of God that is in every single thing, including yourself.

### Was your lifespan determined before you were born?
It had a healing range of time, and I had already gotten toward the middle of it.

### Do you have a message for me to pass along to Robin?
Allow her more time to adjust, and she can read your book. It will help her to see the big picture of life and death.

### Thank you, Marty!

*Allow me to tell you one more thing. All the times we had beer and conversations were some of my happiest lifetime experiences.*

**It was always fun—especially when we had your homemade beer.**

*Ha, Ha. Making it was a lot of work, but I enjoyed it also.*

**Maybe I can sneak some into our soul classroom—I understand you can manifest instantly there.**

*I can, but have lost my interest in Earthly enjoyments. They allowed me to heal in Earth time, but I am healed in eternity now.*

**I'll let you go, but please send me insights to become a successful trader.**

*I already am.*

**Thank you, I thought so. I need all the help I can get.**

*Having an edge is important—not only in trading, but in life by healing your mind.*

## Lynda

**With whom can I speak now?**
*Are you hearing me, Paul? This is your acquaintance, Lynda M.*

**I hear you, Lynda. I was very sorry to read that you had died of cancer in your 30s or 40s.**
*I was about 40 at the time I left the Earth.*

**I always wished I had known you better—and that I didn't sabotage any chances of our having a relationship by saying stupid things.**
*Actually, it is a good thing you did. I would have made your life incredibly different—having an entirely different trajectory.*

**Why did you leave here at such a young age?**
*I was an artist, and the Earth to me was not very beautiful. Now, I can only feel love, and I only see beauty.*

**I am really glad to hear from you.**
*Beauty becomes all that you see if you look for it. Hating all that is not beautiful only creates more for your hating to see.*

**Do we know each other in our soul groups? I had a kind of recognition when I saw you on Earth.**
*How can you feel me in your presence? I am in all that is beautiful, and in all that you love to feel as beauty.*

*As energy bodies, we are in some groups exploring beauty together. Allow all that is beauty a home in your heart and mind.*

**I thought you were beautiful.**
*All beauty can be only in your own perception. My beauty allowed you to see it in your mind.*

**Wow—you are giving me some profound truths.**
*All truths are also beautiful, and all beauty heals your mind.*

**My purpose is to help people to heal on Earth. I write poems and messages, and this is for a book about understanding death.**
*All of your books will heal everyone who reads them, and bring beauty into the world.*

**Would you like me to include your death, or after-death experience?**
*Absolutely—it was magnificent! I healed instantly in my mind, allowing beauty in, in infinite degrees of beautification—actually, allowing God healing love in is the best description.*

**What else can you tell me about it?**
*All beauty came into my head, and all non-beauty left it. I ceased being Lynda, and became all that God intended me to be—allowing all that had been me to heal instantly. All I could ever imagine was instantly in my presence, so I had to focus on healing and beauty.*

*After all I had imagined as beauty was in my presence, actually in and as my presence- it actually was my presence in all the beauty I could imagine, I allowed myself and God to be in Oneness.*

**It sounds perfect.**
*It is perfect, making all of life a perfect dream to heal ourselves in.*

**What is next for you?**
*I will acclimate all I can be to have another lifetime dream, and heal myself in it once again. All can heal— or maybe it won't heal in life, and it can heal in its life-ending moment.*

**Thank you, Lynda.**
*All can be beauty if you look for it.*

# Dad

**Who can I speak with now?**
*Actually, it is your father now. Hello, Paul!*

**Hi, Dad! I was thinking today how I miss our regular dinners—besides Mom's best food in the world, we were able to solve all of the world's problems.**
*Actually, all of those problems are not real. They are illusions allowed into your dream, for you to heal by allowing them a healing instant in the Mind of God.*

*A healing instant in the Mind of God can be an eternity in the mind of a person.*

**What does it take for us to heal our dreams of life?**
*All it takes is for you to allow all in life a lifetime to heal itself, because it will—if it wants to, or not.*

*All not healing in life heals in its last moment as it loses its dream life, and comes back into its awareness of it being a dream.*

**It makes me think that I shouldn't take the world too seriously—I didn't come here to be sick.**
*Allow it to heal, and it allows healing in you- making it a mirror of healing that you are looking into.*

*All you can see in the glass mirror is healing, and an opposite reflection—actually nothing more than a mirror image that is not even on the glass. It is reflected.*

*All heals in you, and you reflect it in the mirror. All heals in you by allowing it to heal, and loving it healing.*

*Healing can be instantaneous, or it can be in a lifetime. All heals in any case though.*

**We are faced with daily pressures and disappointments, and are routinely exposed to disturbing local, national, and international events and crises. Should we see them as healing opportunities? If we do, won't life be smoother because we haven't sunk into despair?**

*Actually, all despair does is distance you from having a healed and peaceful mind.*

**Shouldn't we care about what is going on in the world?**

*Caring can be healing it in your mind with loving intentions, and healed it will be—in your mind. A dream is all in your mind.*

**That makes it clear. All we have to do is practice having healing responses to everything in our life dreams. The best part is that having peaceful minds allows us to manifest our desires, and therefore fewer disturbances—by creating a positive feedback loop.**

*All healing is a feedback loop—healing, or not healing. Healing is a positive loop, and not healing is a negative loop—and the loops are on instant replay, over and over in a person's mind.*

**You can heal yourself, or debilitate yourself simply by changing the input into your mental feedback loop.**

*It always heals if it is positive because God is the energy of healing and loving.*

**I was reading last night that some disturbed spirits did not heal upon death, and remain earthbound as ghosts.**

*All heals in your dream by healing it in your mind. All ghosts are halting love in their minds until they can heal themselves in self-love and self-forgiveness—and you can heal them with loving intentions that are directed to them.*

**We can do the same for living beings in our dream.**

*And healing in the mirror reflects back to you.*

[I started to sign off.]

*I have a lot more to say. Healing allows more healing, and healing energy is God. God heals, and God loves each person.*

*God is what each person has in their essence, making healing come from within themselves.*

*All each one has to do is ideally have a positive, loving response to all they are dreaming in their lifetimes.*

**Why hold onto worries if they are only in our minds, and will disappear the moment we die?**
*Achievement can be a lifetime purpose, but the ultimate achievement is healing your mind.*

*A healed mind has no other achievement goals that it could need to heal because all in its dream and reflection is healed.*

**That is being one with God—loving and allowing.**
*Like a flower in nature, yes.*

**Thank you, Dad! We solved the last remaining world problem.**
*If your mind is healed, there are no more problems.*

# Rich

**Can I speak with Rich?**
*Yes, and I can catch all that is asked, and will answer if I can.*

**How are you, Rich?**
*I am all that God is without the ego demands—meaning ego demands are not God-like.*

**I spoke to Buck from our 1980's drafting room.**
*Affectionately known as Wilburn E. Walters.*

**I speak mostly with dead people and God—at least my meaningful conversations... making me wonder if I am dead too.**
*Well, actually... ha, ha.*

**You had me going there for a second!**
*A bigger energy has surrounded you now. It is allowing me to inform you that all you are writing will heal millions of people in books and other mediums. Healing them heals yourself in many unseen ways.*

**What would you call that "bigger energy"?**
*It appears as a glowing wisp of God, having God's love and healing in it.*

**Can you tell me what it was like when you died?**
*It was actually a gift from God in that moment, allowing all that was unwell in my life to disappear.*

**When I called your office, they said you were on sick leave. I didn't know you were THAT sick.**
*And I didn't expect to leave either. I decided I would exit this lifetime in a most efficient way—while on medical leave to keep my pension benefits for my family.*

**Good for you—or them. I wish I had a pension.**
*Maybe all of your books will become bestsellers, ha, ha.*

**Then what happened?**
*I accepted my fate, meaning that I would die from cancer—not an aggressive cancer, but an aggressive cancer treatment.*

**Were you visited by an angel?**
*Actually, I was, and it made me feel good about my fate.*

**Please continue.**
*I could have continued my life, but it was not in my best interest from my soul's perspective.*

*All I could do was heal myself in those final moments until a light came into my head that was unbelievably intense, but it was good for my healing though. It healed my mind, and my body detached from it, making everything about me only lightness.*

*Initially, I thought that was all there is, but I had more to heal. All of a sudden, I was getting higher and higher above the Earth, and I could feel only lovingness in everything I could hear and see from there.*

*Hearing all of the sounds of nature and of life was the most interesting. I had not heard it all at once like that.*

*Hearing it all at once made me feel alive, and healed.*

*Following my course higher made me notice that feelings I had not healed started entering into my mind—all interrupting my loving, healed state of mind. Finally, they healed as I allowed them to heal.*

*I could detail them, but you can imagine how many, and what kinds of thoughts they were.*

*After I acclimated to having only loving thoughts, a guardian angel came and said it would guide me into my classroom where everything is explained, and we are all tested to make sure we understand.*

**Did you have a Lifetime Review?**
*Actually, I had a Lifetime Review when I was in the hospital, going in and out of consciousness.*

*All I could do was heal my thoughts, and hope they stayed healed after that.*

**What was next?**
*I entered a classroom full of other people I have known in my already large number of lifetimes.*

*I had a feeling that all of them loved me unconditionally, and I had loved myself only conditionally.*

*It was the first lesson in the class. All of the lessons had love as the main theme.*

**Did you go to different classrooms?**
*I am always going from one classroom to another, making this a school of lessons on love—not human love, but God's love humans cannot comprehend.*

**As an architect, can you describe the school?**
*I could only hear and feel the classrooms I was in, and I could also see that they were typical classrooms—meaning as classrooms on Earth are typically built. All of the chairs had only a seat and a back, and the desks had only a medium-sized top. The floor was only light, making all on it suspended.*

*The hallway doors had vision panels for instructors to look in on occasion.*

*A giant blackboard had all of our names on it, and all had an assignment next to them.*

**What was your assignment?**
*Achievement has only Earthly attributes. Describe how God's attributes can be achievements on Earth.*

**Is there an easy answer?**
*Answers can be easy, but living them can be difficult.*

**Did you see many instructors?**
*All have come into the classroom to wish all of us well, and to work with us individually mostly.*

**What are the instructors like?**
*All of them are angels that have human features. A few of them are like elves that are very little.*

**Do you communicate in your minds there, and not with language?**
*All communication is in the mind. All language is for having lessons that need to heal.*

**Do you mean because of things we said or didn't say—to others and ourselves?**

*Exactly right—you said it, ha, ha.*

**Do the instructors have a sense of humor?**
*Absolutely. They have many gifts that they love to share.*

**What else would you like me to know about death, or life?**
*It can be however it fits your sense of loving yourself in it—both in life, and in death's afterlife.*

**Is there a point when you will choose another lifetime?**
*It has already been chosen, and can be in any time period and location I choose. I already chose a lifetime that has only few luxuries—making me want more than I can have—and it hurts me to not have more.*

*I have to accept what I can have and love it, or all of it can be lost—meaning, un-manifested.*

**Will the life lesson be about loving life to manifest your desires?**
*And loving myself to heal my dissatisfaction.*

**Where and when will that lifetime be?**
*It is happening now in the heat of a Middle Eastern region, in a century that has not happened yet in your lifetime perspective.*

**Is it in my future?**
*Yes, it is about a thousand years in your future.*

**Wow—I thought the Earth would be depopulated by then.**

*In your Earth lifetime it will, but in another timeline it will not be as yours is.*

**How are there different timeline realities?**
*All are a dream in the Mind of God, so they are all illusions.*

**How many are there?**
*As many as there are dreamers.*

**So, we do create our entire realities, and universes.**
*Allowing all that you are dreaming a healing experience that can be instantaneous, or it can be an impossible dream.*

**How can I heal instantly... without dying?**
*Allow all that has come into your universe to be a loving reminder that all of it is there to be loved by you.*

**Some of it needs to be despised though.**
*Despising anything makes you a despiser. Your lesson is to be a lover as God intends.*

**That really sums it up.**
*That is the classroom lesson you can skip if you learn it in the Earth classroom.*

**Thank you, Rich! I am glad I reached you—that was very enlightening!**
*Have an enlightening life—until next time!*

**See ya.**
*And all I can see is lovingness.*

## LORIANN

**With whom can I speak next?**
*Hi Paul, all I can do is laugh at your hearing me now. This is Loriann!*

*I am almost alive, just not living in a body now.*

**Yes, I heard that you had died in a car crash about 15 years ago while in another state.**
*I did die, and it was almost my time to leave the planet.*

**Why was it almost your time to leave?**
*I could not leave without saying goodbye to my parents because we were close. All I needed was to be in their company one more time, but I did not get a chance, being far away at the time.*

*Make a flower arrangement for me please, and send it to them.*

**Didn't your Earthly concerns disappear the moment you died?**
*All but having a heavy heart for allowing myself an exit without saying goodbye.*

**I understand that the souls closest to us are also in our soul groups, and don't really leave there. We just initiate illusions of living lifetimes to heal in—so, don't you see them there?**

*I always see them here, and in their Earthly lives—but I want their healing to be more profound in their Earthly lives.*

**I assume they are both alive now?**
*Alive, and always grieving their loss.*

**If I interfere, they may be upset, or reject my outlandish spiritual claims.**
*Can you help me to help them heal please?*

**Okay, I am all about healing, but they will remember me from my college days 45 years ago, as a member of Animal House.**
*I know, how could anyone forget?*

**Yeah, that's what I was afraid of...**
*Actually, it was a lot of fun while it lasted. Can anyone help me heal my parents?*

*All I want is to say how much I want to be near them again.*

**Won't this make them sad?**
*I want you all to know that I am not really dead, and can hear all that you have to say to me!*

**Okay, hang on. I will finish this book right away, and rush it to Maryann and Jenny (mutual friends who are also sisters). They will know how to contact your family.**
*All right!! How can I thank you?*

**Promise me your parents won't be upset, and that this will be a healing experience.**
*I promise it will be healing if they hear me again.*

**How can they be sure it is you?**
*Ask them what my nickname was. It was 'Lor'.*

**Back to my book about death—can you tell me what it was like?**
*I remember a crashing sound like a car wreck, but I was not in the car. I was above it and looking down at it. I imagined that it could have been a bad accident, and did not know that I was in the car.*

**Do you think that your spirit left your body right before the crash?**
*It did—I'm a chicken for that kind of trauma.*

**So, it was definitely painless.**
*Not only painless, it was wonderfully invigorating ecstasy!*

**Did you stay at the accident scene?**
*I heard an ambulance, and then I left the area.*

**Did you know that you had died in the crash?**
*No, I was feeling as good as ever.*

**When did you realize it?**
*After I heard my family crying about me.*

**Your kids?**
*And my husband, and all of my family.*

**Where did you go when you left the accident scene?**
*After I had been around my family members, hoping they could hear that I'm not really dead—I accepted the already obvious conclusion that they cannot hear me.*

*An angel came and held my hand, and told me it was a necessary and healing event for all of them.*

*After I accepted that, it gave me instructions on what we were going to do next—meaning, after I could get the courage to leave the planet.*

*Get ready for this part because it is amazing! All I could feel was God loving me in the most fantastic, complete, and intense way that I didn't want anything else. I ascended higher and higher until I was away from the Earth.*

*I made it to heaven! Another angel came toward me and guided me higher into an incredible lightness.*

*After I arrived in the higher lightness, I came into a large room that had all of the spirits I know in it—having all been notified that I was coming. They gave me an incredible homecoming reception.*

**Was there a period of Lifetime Review?**
*Actually, it came after my homecoming reception. The angel accompanied me to a theater, which was another auditorium-like space. A film had been playing for me to hear and see- not only to hear and see, but to actually be in it again!—and hearing myself from other peoples' perspectives.*

*It could have been worse, but I know how they felt.*

**Then what?**
*I entered another classroom to contemplate what I had learned.*

**Did an instructor come in?**

*An angel came in and gave me confidence and support every so often.*

**When you say, "every so often," is there a sense of having a time sequence there?**
*A sequence, yes—but not in time, only in my mind and energy body having experiences.*

**Does it seem like it has been 15 years since you left the planet?**
*It can be an instant, and it can be an eternity. It depends how attuned I am to Earth time in my mind.*

**What else can you tell me?**
*I am attuned to Earth time now, and can't believe you are in your 60s already!*

**Yup, older and a little wiser—working on my assignments here, exploring consciousness.**
*A long way from the Animal House where you guys had the best parties!*

**I was thinking the same thing.**
*I heard it in your mind, and had to say it for you.*

**About the classrooms there—how do you like the chairs with no legs?**
*I didn't notice until you said it, but you are right—they have no legs! I am hovering like being on an air cushion.*

**How about the blackboard?**
*It has my name on it with my assignments.*

**How many assignments?**

*All have one major assignment, and multiple minor assignments—making my homework the only thing I can do with my mind now.*

**Couldn't you quickly complete the assignments?**
*All have to be completed for every lifetime, and from every person's perspective, so no.*

**Are you the only one in the classroom now?**
*An instructor comes in and gives me guidance often, so other than that, I am.*

**Do you join other soul groups sometimes?**
*Almost every time I complete an assignment, I join some other energy bodies that I know, and also meet new ones that I do not know. I have many angels that help me make decisions also.*

**What kinds of decisions?**
*All decisions I need to make for advancing higher in consciousness—like having another Earthly life as a female, in another location, and in another century if I want it to be.*

**Are you ready to incarnate as a person again?**
*Actually, I am considering it for another planet, yes.*

**Another planet?**
*As a male, and not a female in that life, yes.*

**How many planets do you have to choose from?**
*As a human being, I had 440 to choose from. As another type of being, there are many thousands to choose from.*

**Now I have a lot of questions. When you say, "another type of being," would it be more advanced than a human being?**
*It isn't hard to be more advanced than a human being, but it is hard to be a human being.*

*Humans have conflicts in their minds that make conflicts in their lives.*

**Do the human beings always have male and female genders?**
*Humans have genders to polarize them, and allow them to heal in one more duality of their natures.*

**What planet are you considering to incarnate on?**
*It is a planet in another solar system, named Cilitro.*

**What do you know about it?**
*It is a lot like Earth, but we only have water to breathe. We are underwater. All of the planet is covered with water.*

**People live underwater?**
*All of the animals and plants are underwater, kind of like an aquarium.*

**Is it fresh water?**
*It always has a salt content, but not that much.*

**Are there predator animals there that humans are afraid of?**
*All animals here are friendly, like porpoises on Earth, and all have a diet of vegetation like algae, and a type of Krill.*

**It sounds wonderful. I guess people swim more than walk?**
*They also ask their animal friends to carry them, like you would imagine riding a porpoise.*

**Do they communicate with the animals and fish?**
*There are only animals and no fish, meaning all mammals that do not lay eggs. All communicate with each other in their minds.*

**Are there buildings and towns?**
*There are huge enclaves of homes built from lifting stones into amazing structures that are very artistically built.*

**What do underwater people do there?**
*All are finding their own creative expressions in life, like on the Earth. Mostly they are composing music, or drawing with a kind of paste that illuminates as it is drawn onto anything.*

**Is it deep and dark underwater?**
*It is not especially deep or dark where I will be living, meaning I can always see what I am doing.*

**Is there an atmosphere above the water?**
*Yes, it is almost like the Earth's, but we cannot breathe it for long.*

**What advice can you give to humans who are now living on the Earth?**
*All God has intended for you is all you need to allow into your hearts and minds. Ask God, and God will*

*always answer in the affirmative by directing it to you.*

**I almost forgot—at the beginning, you said that it was almost your time to leave the planet. Was your lifespan pre-determined?**
*Yes, and I decided not to have it changed.*

**Why not?**
*I had agreed to it, along with everyone else in my life around me.*

**Thank you, Loriann! I will see to it that your parents receive your messages and story.**
*And I thank you, from the endless bottom of my heart.*

**Here is a snip of one of those party invitations.**
*Ha, ha, ha, I love that memory of your large hair-do, making a hair-don't!... and having hair is an accomplishment now.*

**You took my thought again.**
*Actually, I didn't—but I guessed it was in your thoughts.*

**Bye for now, Loriann!**
*Achievement in life can be a hair loss memory also— having it will mean losing it.*

**Well, that's a downer.**
*Having life means having it eternally, so it is not a downer for long.*

*Achievement is having God's love in your heart and mind.*

## Billy & John

**Who is next to contribute to my fascinating accounts of leaving the Earth by dying?**
*Both Billy and John Haverly want to have words in the book for when you contact their sisters, Maryann and Jenny.*

**Perfect timing—I was hoping to hear from you now.**
*A few words is all we want to have, now that Loriann said so much.*

**You guys left the planet early also. No doubt it was very difficult for your family.**
*Life can be difficult, and we had difficult Earth lifetimes. Leaving the Earth is not difficult, and can be the best part of the whole experience of living in a body.*

**What did you find difficult about living on Earth?**
*This is John—always being loved, but not loving myself as much as I should have, and allowing myself to hurt my family in my acts of self-destruction—and please let them know that I am truly sorry.*

**I will.**
*This is Billy. All I can add is all we need is love, as the Beatles sang about.*

*How can life not be all about love if we come from God? It can be, only if a life is not aligned with God— and not aligned with God means we are only dreaming it all to heal ourselves back into alignment with God.*

**Well said.**
*"Healing back into alignment with God" is another way of describing death, and death is the end of the dream that we are not aligned with God.*

**We are God.**
*Individual Gods in individual dreams, in a collective dream.*

**Until we wake up from the dream by seeing only Love/ God/ Oneness.**
*Actually, that heals you in your individual dream, and changes the collective dream to be a dream of life that you would love the most.*

**I like it... I mean, I love it.**
*Love is all there is, and lack of love is all there is not. If you love life by loving yourself in it, you are creating a dream universe in that feeling, because that feeling is God. Without God, you cannot create anything.*

**There are plenty of godless creatures here trying to ruin everything.**
*They cannot create, only destroy—and they cannot destroy you because you are God having a dream.*

*They cannot create anything.*

**That's a great way to look at it, and it eliminates any fears that I have.**
*All fear cancels love, and manifests what you are afraid of. Love allows your desires to manifest by aligning all desires with God, and allows illusory fears to disappear.*

**Thank you, Billy and John! Do you have anything else to add?**
*Nothing your other guests haven't already told you.*

**How about a message for your sisters Maryann and Jenny, and your brother Patrick?**
*Ask all of them to forgive me. This is John.*

*Billy here—make each of them a heart-shaped note asking them to feel only love in their hearts and minds—for me, and for all of life. It will heal them more than they can imagine.*

**I trust that you have seen your parents again?**
*Actually, here they are now to add to this message:*

*"Each of us had to find our own courage, and all of you were fearless in living, and allowing dying to be part of it."*

**Thank you, Mr. and Mrs. H!**
*Thank you, Paul. We are happy that you can hear us and will share these messages with our other children.*

**You can hear them if they talk to you, correct?**
*Always, and anything they have to tell us is encouraged and welcomed.*

**I'll tell you something—you were kind people, and your Christmas parties were the best!**
*As 'the hosts of Christmas past', we always had a wonderful time allowing everyone a gathering to express their love of life.*

**Ha! "The hosts of Christmas past" without the 'g' in "hosts." That's hilarious!**
*A comic relief for Maryann, Jenny, and Patrick when they read this.*

## Peter Giampietro & Mr. Coe

**Who will be next?**
*Hi, allow me to have this forum for giving your readers a laugh also, making a book of light-hearted conversations about death. This is a friend from a long time ago, and a classmate, Peter Giampietro.*

**Hi, Peter.**
*Hi, Paul. We did not know each other that well in grade school, but all I have to add is a light-hearted comment.*

**Let's hear it!**
*A life can be all you have intended for it, so always be inventively intentive!*

**Good one, Peter!**
*I saw Mr. Coe here. He is in your main soul group.*

**I have known that he is in my primary soul group. He was our very kind and funny woodshop and art teacher.**
*He painted my portrait for my parents, and helped make all of my projects special.*

*He is here, and has a few things he can help you with now.*

**Hello, Mr. Coe!**
*Hello, Paul. I can hear you like when you were my student, working on creatively expressing yourself—like me.*

*Creatively expressing yourself means healing your heart and mind, and allowing God as love to come through you.*

*After that heart healing, and mind feeling, 'all you can be' is God.*

**Thank you, Mr. Coe. Since we are in the same primary soul group of 5 souls, we incarnate in the same lifetimes routinely.**
*All are healing for both of us, and God can express itself as individuals in a dream having non-love in it.*

**How would you describe God?**
*God is 'all there is' having a dream allowing 'all there is' to illuminate and heal 'all that is not'.*

**I think I understand it—only love or God is real; all non-love is not God, so it must be an illusion. To be like God, I have to either love it or allow it. If I fight against illusions, I will only be suffering in my own mind, and not healing.**
*All certainly cannot heal if you are not loving or allowing all of it in your mind. All God can be in life is loving and allowing.*

**When I am loving and allowing, I am really allowing God Mind in my mind, which is then manifesting my desires... and when I'm not, I'm not.**
*Correct—have you forgotten one important point?*

**To love myself because I am love from God?**

*'All there is' cannot heal 'all that is not' without loving itself—making 'all God is' complete in all of its healed splendor.*

**Like animals and nature. Nothing in nature hates life or hates itself.**
*All God can do is express itself as loving life and itself in all life.*

**I have a question about the spirit world. What is it like looking at our physical world in time? I picture it as if you are looking out of an airplane window—but you are not moving, and we appear to be moving by on the ground below.**
*Actually, that is a good way to envision our perspective here, and each airplane window is a different lifetime of ours.*

*A window will illuminate if there is a loving connection being made, as it illuminates now for all who have known you in your life, and have also died.*

**I would like readers to know that deceased loved ones and pets can hear their loving communications, and will greet them at the moment they pass away also.**
*An aching heart can also be heard by their loved ones, and their loved ones heal it with the help of angels.*

**Pets are in heaven also, correct?**
*A loving, healing animal companion will always be with each person eternally.*

**What is the function of angels?**

*Angels allow God Mind access to your mind, and accessing God Mind is all you could ever hope for because it is 'all there is'.*

### As an artist, how would you describe angels?
*Angels are like a rainbow after a storm, and a birdsong in the springtime. Angels illuminate in fluorescent colors that can only be described as like cotton candy in multiple colors. They are as beautiful as any being can be, and have wings to maneuver in higher consciousness.*

### What advice can you give to me and the readers of this book?
*Achieving healing is not hard when connecting to God Mind. It can be hard if not allowing God Mind in hope, love, and patience every moment.*

### Thank you, Mr. Coe!
*Call on angels for hope, love, and patience in your mind, and all will be loving in your life.*

## Loriann Again

**Lor, are you there?**
*I am, and have a lot more to explain about heaven. All that heaven is will always be a little different for each person, and heaven is in their love of life at all times.*

**Is heaven in rings of consciousness that are around the Earth at the line of night and day—so that we are passing under the rings at sunrise and sunset as they sweep across the planet?**
*Actually, I have to ask my instructors. I don't know where heaven is in relation to each planet.*

**Are you able to ask now?**
*I asked, and my angel instructor folded its wings to hold me as we ascended higher and higher into the lightness. God is in heaven along with all of the ascended masters that we heard about.*

*All God and the ascended masters can do is love.*

*All love can do is allow itself illumination, and illumination allows itself to be in a darkened illusion—meaning illuminating a dream of illusory darkness.*

**That would be here on Earth—a dream of light and dark.**
*Love and non-love can only be dreamt if you are love, allowing non-love to exist.*

**Did God and the ascended masters acknowledge you?**
*I allowed God and the ascended masters to heal my mind and heart, and my angel held me as I illuminated in all love and wisdom, healed in all peacefulness.*

**Will you go back to your classroom now?**
*Angelic wisdom has elevated me to be a spirit guide for souls that are arriving here.*

**I am sure that you will make them feel comfortable and welcome.**
*A guide can help them to accept their elevated circumstance, and to control their thoughts because they manifest instantly here.*

**How does that work? If you imagine being a tiger on the Earth, would you become a tiger?**
*I would become a tiger in my mind, but I do not have a healing need for it.*

**Don't some spirits inadvertently manifest what they don't want?**
*All can manifest their desires, mainly for healing—a lot like on the Earth, but instantly.*

**About your school classroom—what would you see if you went out of the door and down the hall?**
*I will go into the hallway now. I am in it, and there are more classrooms on both sides.*

*All have students in them, and many have only one student.*

**Can you go to the end of the hallway, and go outside?**
*I am going, and it is a long hallway. I am going outside now.*

*How can it be that there is no building here? There is only lightness enveloping me.*

*I am back inside now—that is not what I expected.*

*I expected a building with a lot of windows and a courtyard area. I am going back to my classroom now to contemplate healing in a school of only lightness.*

**I guess that's it—you are in a school of lightness, and I'm in a school of lightness and darkness.**
*All heals in lightness, so going to a school in darkness has many more healing challenges to experience.*

**Can I affirm that I am healed, and that I will love and allow everything—so I won't get any challenges in darkness?**
*All heals in your loving and allowing it—so allow only love, and love is what heals you.*

**Can you see the future at all for my timeline on Earth?**
*I can always hear, feel, and see what I allow myself to hear, feel, and see.*

**Are there multiple realities and timelines that we each will branch off into, or are we all on the same train heading down the track?**

*All are on the same train having an adventure, and healing in each of the train cars is a different experience for every passenger.*

**I could choose to be in the Club Car with a great view, but... here's my question—is the train about to crash?**
**It's going extremely fast, trees are falling on the track, bridges are crumbling, and the engineer driver is a maniac.**
*A crash can be a good way for everyone to heal themselves into the light at the same time. All can hop off at any time also.*

**'The light at the end of the tunnel' could be an oncoming train.**
*Actually, "the light at the end of the tunnel" is heaven in infinite lightness where there are no tracks, and healing is all you will experience.*

**Is there an ETA for us to jump the tracks?**
*It has different arrival times for each person. Check your ticket.*

**I'm going back to the Club Car.**
*I am going back into my classroom to help a new arrival here.*

**Bye, Loriann! "One more thing," as Lieutenant Colombo would say. You commented on the photo I found from a college party invitation. Could you see it?**

*I could hear, feel, and see what you were hearing, feeling, and seeing at that moment because I acclimated to your mind.*

### How can your family connect with you?
*All they have in their minds I can acclimate to also if they are healing, loving thoughts.*

### Do you have a message for them?
*I am always hearing their healing, loving thoughts about me, and I'm hoping they hear me when they allow this information to heal their minds.*

### Bye again, Loriann!
*I can hear what you are thinking, so do not fear for your future. It is always determined by yourself, and no one else.*

### Thank you for that.
*All is my pleasure here.*

# Eric

**Do I know someone who has died and is having another lifetime several generations in our future, or can tell me what it is like, say in 97 years—or in the year 2121?**
*Achievement is halted and humanity will be extinct in another 50 years.*

**Who is this?**
*It is a classmate, Eric. You did not know I had died in my early 50s. I acclimated to hearing your other guests, and wanted to add to your knowledge of human consciousness.*

*Achievement in life has many meanings, and what I meant was achievement in ingenuity, not in healing by God instilling loving thoughts in them.*

**Destructive capabilities are part of humanity's growing ingenuity.**
*Correct, and hating has its limits, as does everything except God's love.*

**Will humanity destroy itself, or will the Earth shake them off in a geomagnetic reversal?**
*All humans come to Earth with a timeline they agreed to, to have healing opportunities in.*

*Not healing in life heals in death, healing all the same.*

Earth timelines are not being agreed to after about 48 more years. An era ends, and a new era begins.

**So, the poles flip, and the Earth becomes cooler?**
And cataclysms alter the geography and oceans dramatically. The Earth has no more humans because of the intense level of cosmic rays that are allowed entry when the magnetic field of protection weakens, and the Earth starts to rotate in the opposite direction.

**Are you having an Earth lifetime during that period?**
I already had it, meaning it was in my past and in your future.

**Wow—so you lived it already. What was your life like then?**
It allowed me to heal my fear of failure when I heroically acted altruistically, and gave my healing water to others that needed it.

**Was it hard to find clean water?**
It has been hard to find clean water from the time of your life in about 10 more years.

**What contaminates it?**
A large and deadly cloud of radiation will envelope the Earth in a nuclear holocaust.

**I thought that the nuclear warheads were all disabled beyond repair by light beings.**[2]

---

[2] Explained in my book, *Mysteries, Prophecies, and the Hollow Earth*.

*All have been, but another one is being made in China right now.*

**US Intelligence Says China Leading 'Rapid Expansion' Of Nuclear Arsenal**

Defense Intelligence Agency: China on track to have **over 1,000 operational nuclear warheads by 2030**.

SAT OCT 26, AT 10:45 PM     👁 13,641   💬 171

**Can I ask the light beings to disable it?**
*Have it disabled, and you will save humanity from that timeline possibility.*

**If you already lived that timeline in my future, and I change it now—does reality branch off into another timeline?**
*It always branches off into 5 more timelines, one for each of your timelines there.[3]*

**Where were you living in that lifetime?**
*I already had my lifetime there, but it was in an eastern Himalayan town of Tibet.*

**How did you get clean water?**
*It came from a spring underground, having no contact with the Earth atmosphere.*

**Thank you, Eric! I need to contact the light beings. Believe it or not, they live inside of the Earth.**
*I know. Halting the Earth's destruction is their main focus now—to have a planet they can inhabit also.*

---

[3] Explained in my book *The 4 Secrets of the Universe*.

🅰 https://americanmilitarynews.com › 2021 › 06 › ufos-took-us-nuclear-systems-offline-repeate...

**UFOs took US nuclear systems offline repeatedly, former Pentago...**

In a Tuesday interview with the Washington Post, Luis Elizondo, the former director of the Pentagon's Advanced Aerospace Threat Identification Program (AATIP), said unidentified flying objects (UFOs) repeatedly rendered U.S. nuclear capabilities inoperable.

https://www.prnewswire.com › news-releases › former-usaf-officers-to-present-evidence-of-...

**Former USAF Officers to present evidence of UFOs Tampering wit...**

RSVP: Robert Salas salasrobe@protonmail.com (805) 294 5154. Contact: Robert Salas. (805) 294 5154. SOURCE Former USAF Officers Present Evidence of UFOs Tampering with Nuclear Weapons.

Ⓜ https://www.mirror.co.uk › news › weird-news › ten-nuclear-warheads-switched-off-29294059

**Ten nuclear warheads 'switched off' by nearby UFOs, investigators...**

Feb 23, 2023 — Former US Air Force intercontinental ballistic missile launch officer Robert Salas has testified he was on duty at Malmstrom air force base in Montana on March 24, 1967, when an orange disc-shaped ...

Ⓒ https://www.cbsnews.com › news › ex-air-force-personnel-ufos-deactivated-nukes

**Ex-Air Force Personnel: UFOs Deactivated Nukes - CBS News**

Ex-Air Force Personnel: UFOs Deactivated Nukes. September 28, 2010 / 10:33 AM EDT / CBS ... told of several occasions having to go out and "re-start" missiles that had been deactivated, after UFOs ...

---

**PR Newswire** | News | Products | Contact

News in Focus   Business & Money   Science & Tech   Lifestyle & Health   Policy & Public Interest   People & Culture

# Former USAF Officers to present evidence of UFOs Tampering with Nuclear Weapons

Former officers call on the U.S. Congress to hold public hearings

NEWS PROVIDED BY
Former USAF Officers Present Evidence of UFOs Tampering with Nuclear Weapons →
Oct 07, 2021, 10:28 ET

SHARE THIS ARTICLE

OJAI, Calif., Oct. 7, 2021 /PRNewswire/ -- Declassified U.S government documents and witness testimony from former or retired U.S. Air Force personnel to be presented as evidence of ongoing incursions by unidentified aerial objects at nuclear missile sites over several decades. These will be cited to support the claim that nuclear missiles were inexplicably disabled while a UAP object silently hovered nearby. Four former officers involved in such encounters will discuss these and other incidents at the National Press Club and urge the U.S. Congress to investigate and hold public hearings.

# Lulo

**I would like to connect with a representative from the inner-earth.**
*Hello, this is Lulo from the Earth's interior. Allow me to assist you in any way that I can.*

**Hello again, Lulo. I have some news from someone who has lived in my future.**
**He said that a nuclear bomb is being built in China that will detonate, causing a nuclear winter in about 10 more years.**
*I am alarmed, but not actually surprised.*

*All human hatred has an ending that is not in the best interest of anyone on the planet.*

*All I can do is halt another ending by disabling the nuclear missile completely, meaning it cannot destroy anyone or anything.*

**Thank you very much, Lulo. Are you also working to move the magnetic North Pole, which is accelerating in its repositioning?**
*Allowing the Earth to heal itself in a new era devoid of humans, yes.*

**This and more is detailed in my recent books—hundreds of messages from God, the inner-earth, Andromeda, and the devil itself. Will my information be too late?**

*All will heal in their minds who read your books by creating alternate timelines into futures of infinite healing potential—by allowing it in life, and inevitably healing in the moment they decide it is finished.*

https://www.nature.com › articles › d41586-019-00007-1
**Earth's magnetic field is acting up and geologists don't know why**
The magnetic pole is moving so quickly that it has forced the world's geomagnetism experts into a rare move. ... And the fast motion of the north magnetic pole could be linked to a high-speed ...

https://science.howstuffworks.com › environmental › earth › geophysics › earths-magnetic-n...
**Earth's Magnetic North Pole Has Rapidly Shifted in the Past 40 Years**
About 55 kilometers (34 miles) annually. "It didn't move much between 1900 and 1980, but it's really accelerated in the past 40 years," geophysicist Ciaran Beggan told Reuters on Friday, Jan. 11. Scientists aren't exactly sure why the magnetic pole has picked up speed although it looks like a jet of liquid iro...

https://www.nature.com › articles › s41561-020-0570-9
**Recent north magnetic pole acceleration towards Siberia caused b...**
The wandering of Earth's north magnetic pole, the location where the magnetic field points vertically downwards, has long been a topic of scientific fascination. Since the first in situ ...

https://phys.org › news › 2019-12-world-magnetic-north-pole-siberia.html
**Updated World Magnetic Model shows magnetic north pole contin...**
The newly updated model shows the magnetic north pole moving away from Canada and toward Siberia. The magnetic north pole is the point on the Earth that compasses designate as true north. It is

## Loriann, Billy & John

**Loriann, are you there?**
*I am always here, and can always hear.*

**Sorry it's taking so long to get this book done for your family—it's been 3 weeks since we last communicated. It won't be long now, maybe a week.**
*Yes, it will be about another week.*

**I just published *The 4 Secrets of the Universe* this week, and started writing the next book of messages from people that I did not know, and who have died. The first message is from David Bowie. He died of cancer 8 years ago, at age 69. He said that he got bored, and was telling me about "creativity without limits."**
*He calculated his creations for their effect. Creativity can have no effect other than healing its creator and the observer.*

**You must be a very advanced soul to be a spirit guide now.**
*I am about halfway healed in the Mind of God.*

**David Bowie may be totally healed. It sounded like he is enlightened now.**
*He is enlightened in creating an enlightened state, as he is healing in God Mind also.*

**What would you like to say? It's 3 AM, so I thought I'd add another chapter.**
*I beckoned you in your sleep, and you woke up.*

**You beckoned me in my sleep? Isn't that illegal?**
*Haaa haaa haaa! I legally beckoned, ha, ha, ha.*

*Good morning, I am calling and leaving you a voicemail message on your hearing aid app that picks up my every beck and call. Your hearing me has healed me in my energy heart center, alternating healing and healed in the Mind of God.*

**This is a total change of topic, but I got another message saying that spirits are not incarnating on the Earth in about 50 more years because humanity dies off, and that we really are near the end of the human era.**
*Actively heal your Earth timeline, and create a healed Earth timeline as you imagine it can be, meaning as you create it to be.*

**What do you recommend—say, for a life of peace and harmony, prosperity and good health?**
*Have them as an ideal in your mind, and have them illuminate in hopeful, loving thoughts.*

*Allow them to become your healed future in each present moment.*

*Each healed moment in the present is your healed future moments.*

*All healed future moments are alternating from a healed moment now, or in the future's healed past.*

**I guess the only thing that would ruin it is fear.**
*Exactly. Fear is the loss of creative focus, but it can create what you fear.*

**Everyone will have a different outcome, and not everyone will suffer—but are we still near the end of the collective dream of life?**
*A collective dream has billions of dreamers, each having an individual dream that flows into the collective dream.*

*The collective dream changes, depending on its flowers.*

**IMO, media brainwashing engines have been deployed against humanity to make people feel powerless, disillusioned, divided, and dissatisfied—not exactly uplifting humanity.**
*A collective dream can become a collective drain on humanity's goodness, not creating for the good of all in the dream.*

**It seems very dark to me, and that little can be done to turn it around... talk about powerlessness.**
*A little can be done—you can uplift your own dream of a life to be a dream life, meaning it doesn't matter what other people are manifesting for themselves.*

**True, and they cannot manifest for me, so I will not be adversely affected by their miscreations.**

*All can heal in your dream life if you allow it to heal, meaning nothing in your life will create disillusionment or division, dissatisfaction or powerlessness.*

**DDD & P. Can you please give me steps for readers to take that will heal their dream lives, and will avoid the dreaded DDD & P?**
*Here they are—heal your life by doing only 3 things:*

*#1 Decide that healing your mind is your number one priority.*

*#2 Follow your heart's desire in creating only what brings you happiness.*

*#3 Avoid all negativity—including all people, broadcasts, and news stories that do not make you feel empowered.*

**Okay, and spending time in nature would also satisfy them.**
*All in nature activates God's healing in your mind and body.*

*God's healing in your mind and body acclimates God Mind in your mind.*

*God Mind in your mind allows more healing, and so on.*

**God Mind in our minds wakes us up from the dream.**

*God Mind in your mind is like Dorothy healed in* The Wizard of Oz *movie when she has awakened in her home.*

**I wrote a poem about that in my book, *Poems of Life, Love, and the Meaning of Meaning*.**

### DOROTHY GALE

The witch was her ego
   out of control
bent on destroying
   the truth she held close

her truth was Toto
   the scarecrow her mind
to help her get home
   which they set out to find

discovering her heart
   gentle and kind
corroded and stuck
   having lost its shine

out came her courage
   which admitted through tears
after chasing her truth
   that it had only fears

together they went off
   and followed her thoughts
all little people
   certain she's lost

to find a higher power
the Wizard of Oz
exposed as a fraud
  by her truth as a dog

apples and poppies
  and ego demands
an ego determined
  to sabotage their plans

her higher self Glenda
  softly pointed out
that the heart-shaped slippers
  are what she's raging about

don't give them up
  to the ego's control
stand in your power
  by connecting your soles

but flying monkeys
  of guilt and regret
the ego sent out
  to get her and her pet

they tore up her mind
  and damaged her heart
couldn't hold her truth
  and let her courage depart

Dorothy was doomed
  and scheduled to die
to lose her power
  and didn't know why

    but her courage got behind
        as her mind made a plan
    how to save Dorothy
        while the hourglass ran

    diminished by water
        as life in the flow
    the ego was finished
        no one missed it go

    Dorothy got home
        but was surprised to see
    that she had never left
        and her life was a dream

    this is the tale
        of her crossing the veil
    the life and the death
        of Dorothy Gale

*Dorothy died in the movie? I did not know that.*

**That's my interpretation anyway. I mean, she got hit in the head by a window, and then her house dropped about 300 feet.**
*Good point, and her dog did not die though.*
**Here is the most important spiritual concept that you can explain. We came to Earth in a dream for an imaginary length of time—so, we couldn't have left the spirit world—meaning we are all still there.**
**It's like when Dorothy goes "home" at the ending of the movie. She wakes up from her**

dream and is surprised to see that her family is there, and that she had never left.
*Actually, the spirit world is in your mind, so you can never leave it.*

**The spirit world is in our minds? What about the rings of consciousness around the Earth?**
*The Earth hologram is in your mind also, because you are projecting a hologram of the universe.*

**Where am I then?**
*You and I are each an aspect of God, individualized for only one purpose—to find God in all things, or to allow them to heal.*

*Healed in the Mind of God means becoming one with God again. All can find their way back to God in their dreams.*

*All can also dream that they are allowing godlessness to heal.*

**Can anything be godless?**
*All evil, demon-controlled humans are godless creatures, having no love in themselves.*

**Yeah, they've pretty much taken over the planet hologram.** *The 4 Secrets of the Universe* **details that, and it has messages from Lucifer about the demon activities. Lucifer says that demons are not evil, but they are attracted to hateful violence.**
**The demons see an energy implosion and rush to it, basically amplifying the hate, and turning off the love in peoples' minds.**

**Lucifer said that the Earth is "a giant, entertaining hate festival now," leaving it in "hateful bliss."**
*A demon can hijack a person's mind if it enjoys hateful violence. Hating life makes a demon attraction that cannot be healed without loving one's self, to illuminate the mind so the demon has no choice but to leave.*

**If we love life and love ourselves, the demons and demon-controlled people cannot affect us. Higher frequencies flow outward like light, and keep lower frequencies away.**
*Higher frequencies are light, and darkness disappears, having no existence in it.*

**All you have to do is love life and love yourself to have no darkness adversely affect you.**
*"Adversely" means in a way that you do not desire. Your 'Book of Manifesting' has all the details of how a healed mind manifests its desires.*

**My desire is to make books that raise consciousness, and help other people to heal—your family and the Haverlys in particular.**
*Billy and John Haverly are here again.*

*Hello again, Paul. This is Billy. Call on our brother Patrick, and our sisters Maryann and Jenny as quickly as you can please. All of this information will heal them tremendously.*

Roger that. I connected with Patrick on Facebook this week, and am already connected as Friends with Maryann and Jenny.

They will be the first ones to know about this book, and I will urge them to get it immediately. I can't say anything about the content before that, because I noticed that people avoid me after they find out I have spirit conversations.

*Hi, Paul. This is John. I have to laugh at your comment. All people have spirit communication, or they could not be having a dream that they are not in the spirit world. All communication to your spirit is like an air hose to a deep-sea diver.*

*You would not last long without it.*

**You might even get beckoned in your sleep.**

*Ha, ha. Loriann is beckoning you again.*

*I am back, laughing at your un-seriousness. Fun heals in the mind, and in the heart mind—which is in the mind of the spirit.*

*Fun can heal in your entire dream which is supposed to be fun.*

**Is our dream life supposed to be fun, like a challenging game?**

*It most certainly is fun, and is always a game of love—making it God's game of hide-and-seek, except all that is hidden is inside of yourself. Allow all that is inside of your heart to express itself, and the game is won in every play. "Every play" means every moment, every day, every conversation, and in every creative healing act that you can do.*

**Thank you, Loriann. Those are words to live by—words I got beckoned with in the middle of the night.**
*Ha, ha, ha. I will beck-on you again when you are least expecting it!*

**I'll be beckoning your family and the Haverlys in about a week—and need you to back up my beckoning.**
*Because beckoning becomes better between backing beckoners, I'll begin beckoning the bunch before becoming belligerent about your belated beckoning.*

**Groannn... Time for breakfast. I know you can't become belligerent.**
*I can become anything I imagine myself becoming, and that is only love.*

**The comments above are for entertainment purposes only.**
*Life can be fun, in a game of hide-and-seek for the love inside yourself.*

**If the universe is in my mind, and also in your mind, then where are you?**
*I am everywhere, meaning not in the hologram anymore. All not in the hologram is in God Mind as an aspect of God that is healing or healed, depending on how acclimated in alignment it is in oneness with Oneness, or God Mind.*

**Our holograms of life are just projections of twoness.**
*In infinite degrees of separation from God, allowing you to motion back to God in only one way—by loving all of life, and allowing all that is not aligned with God Mind to heal in your hologram.*

**If I love and allow all that is in my projected hologram, then there won't be any place for darkness.**
*Actually, there is never a place for darkness in a light hologram, unless you imagine that there is.*

**I get it—evil and non-love are not in God Mind, so they are only illusions in my dream.**
*All healing in your dream of love and non-love are healing illuminations that allow God perpetual illumination.*

**What if people don't heal and illuminate—how would God illumination perpetuate itself?**
*It allows all in its creation a chance to love itself. If nothing loved itself, then God would become a light that has no properties, meaning a light that does not illuminate life.*

*Life is not possible without light, so there would be no life—meaning God cannot be without life, and it could not love itself in that case anyway.*

*All God can do is love and allow—and asking, "What does it love and allow?" answers, "All that there is"— which is only love.*

*Love is all there is, so it cannot NOT love itself.*

*It can love, and it can allow all that heals in love—making a circular feedback loop of loving and allowing.*

**A poem from my book *The Lightness of Being* comes to mind.**
*All you have written in your poetry and other books heal in the minds of those who read them.*

### IT DEPENDS WHAT YOU SEE

>Some spiritual texts
>  say evil doesn't exist
>there is only love
>  or a lack of this
>
>and lack is a perception
>  a mental deception
>it was not created
>  or a part of conception
>
>What you see
>  is what you get
>a feedback loop
>  that's always set
>
>by your intention
>  and love attention
>the clever part
>  of our invention
>
>is that it begins with you
>  and ends with me
>or the other way around
>  it depends what you see

**I want to get more information for your family. Are you greeting souls that are arriving to the spirit world after they have physically died on Earth?**
*Actually, I am guiding all of the souls I knew on the Earth, especially my family.*

**Do you hear their thoughts and needs, and whisper answers to them, or visit them in dreams?**
*All of the above, meaning yes, and yes. I can do all of that and more, helping to heal their minds.*

*Ask them to ask me anything, and I will help them with an answer.*

**Okay. I'd also like to know more about your environment. Before you were in a spirit classroom. What is it like around you if you are everywhere?**
*All that is around me heals in my imagining them around me.*

**What is around you now?**
*Actually, I am not around anything now because I am focusing on your questions.*

*I can hear and feel what you are thinking... not beckoning, just hearing.*

**Ha, ha... you knew what I was thinking.**
*I did, and it was funny that you had that thought.*

**Please tell me more about your experience now. Do your thoughts manifest your desires instantly?**
Actually, my thoughts are about healing my family, and I am acclimating to your mind so you will help me.

**Do you see angels?**
Angels are higher than what I am looking at, but I have met many.

**What are they like?**
Angels are like what you can imagine them to look like, except they are all lightness. A light being that has only light features is a beautiful being.

**They are beautiful beings with wings, correct?**
An angel has a pair of wings to fly higher in consciousness with, and connect to God Mind.

**We picture "higher" as in the 'up' direction, but you mean higher in vibration—and it cannot be in a direction if you are everywhere.**
All that heals is higher, and all that doesn't heal is lower in consciousness.

**When you were in the spirit classroom, and sitting in a chair looking at a blackboard—did you feel like you had a body also?**
A body has limits to it. I do not have any limits, being an energy being now.

**What is your point of reference if you are no longer in a body, a lifetime, a planet hologram, etc.?**

*All I am referencing is all that I love, and that is my family.*

**Will your sisters, Mary and Patty be open to receiving these messages?**

*All of my family members will hear my voice in these messages from my energy body, and I can amplify it in their hearts and minds.*

*Ask my sisters if they can feel my presence when they have loving thoughts about me.*

**I'm sure they will feel your presence, and will be comforted in knowing that you are only gone from your physical limitations—or more accurately, that all of us are only temporarily gone from our real home in the spirit world.**

**I hope that your parents, husband, kids, and friends find this comforting also.**

*All death means is waking up and becoming aware that we were dreaming.*

**Bye, Loriann.**
*Bye, Paul. Beck, beck.*

## Afterword

We learn a lot about life and healing from animals—from their patience, loyalty, courage, unconditional love, and honesty with feelings.

The excerpt below is from my book, *Infinite Healing: Poems and Messages for the Loss of Your Animal Companion*.

I am asking questions to God Mind here.

**Do our animal companions stay around us in spirit after they die?**
*Yes, allowing them another way to heal their human companions in timelessness.*

**Do animals not need to learn lessons of love and self-love, forgiveness, guilt and shame?**
*Animals all work to teach humanity more than they learn in their incarnations.*

**What are their most important teachings?**
*Allowing flowing of life and loving it in each moment, healing others in time.*

**Unconditionally allowing love, life, and loss of life.**
*All motion means half healing in life's motion, and half moving and living in gratitude.*

*All life allows more life and healing in time.*

**Could my pet always know my feelings?**
*All minds opening in love know each other.*

**Are animals afraid of death?**
*Instincts allow survival, love allows death.*

**Will my pet in spirit come to me in dreams to bring me peace?**
*All motioning in light, illuminating in dreams, healing in the mind, yes.*

**Did my animal companion teach me what unconditional love is?**
*No, the love healing in your mind allowed your animal to open it, healing the mind.*

**I hear a bird singing outside. They don't hold onto negative thoughts, do they?**
*All healing in each moment and each loving song, no.*

**Will I see my pet again at the end of my life?**
*Yes, other pets and relatives will meet you also.*

## God's Only Plan

I guess that's it
   I'll never see you again
or maybe I will
   and that will be when

we'll both look back
   saying "wasn't that grand!"
a dream of love or lack
   then to understand

there is only one
   from infinite views
God's only plan
   was for us to choose

From my book, *Infinite Healing: Poems and Messages for the Loss of a Loved One*

"*Birth in the physical is the death in the spiritual. Death in the physical is the birth in the spiritual.*"

—*Edgar Cayce*

## About the Author

From God Mind:

*Paul Gorman illuminates as a spiritual researcher,
writing his discoveries into books,
allowing healing in the minds
of all who read them.*

www.ingramcontent.com/pod-product-compliance
Lightning Source LLC
Chambersburg PA
CBHW030555080526
44585CB00012B/383